Other Books by Fred Sterling

Kirael: The Great Shift
Also published in German

Kirael Volume II: The Genesis Matrix
Also published in Finnish

Guide to the Unseen Self
Also published in German

Kirael: The Ten Principles of Consciously Creating

The Ten Principles of Conscious Creation – Official Textbook
Also published in Hebrew
eBook version available in Spanish

Creator and Me: A Lightworker's Prayers for Meditation and Healing

These and audio recordings of live Kirael sessions, prayers and meditations

available at: www.kirael.com

or call:

+1 800 390-1886

Kirael
THE
GREAT SHIFT
Revised Edition

by

Fred Sterling

Honolulu, Hawaii USA

Kirael: The Great Shift
Revised Edition

By
Fred Sterling

ISBN: 978-0-9675353-5-7

First published in 1998 in paperback by Oughten House Publications
Original ISBN: 1-880666-76-6
Lightways Publishing ISBN: 0-9675353-6-0

Honolulu, Hawaii

Email: lightways@kirael.com
Website: www.kirael.com/lightways

Cover Art: Lance Agena
Layout and Design: Sylvia D'Andrea
Author Photo: Preston Terada

Contents

Acknowledgments

To each who volunteered to bring forth this gift of healing I say, "Thank you from my heart. Thank you for your one hundred percent. Thank you for your Truth, Trust and Passion. Thank you for your willingness to experience. All will know the depth of your contributions to the healing of Mother Earth upon your return to the Creator."

The Original Team: Hokuau, Lauren, Vicky, Lance Agena, Sue Afaga Bowman, Karen E. Boyle, Linda R. Carlson, Gerald Hugh de Heer, Lori Domingo, Tracey H. Edmundson, Roscoe 0. Ford, Mahina Gipaya, Bruce Gorst, Kehau Handa, Sherri-Anne M.Q. Kamaka, Gail Jan Kaneshiro, Phillip M.K. Lau, Stacie T. Lau, Gail M. Lum, Donn Marutani, Mel Morishige, Akihiro Moriwaki, Valerie Moriwaki, Weilynn R. Omori, Marissa Paulino, Lisa Ann Quizon, Marni Suu Reynolds, Paul Wayne Richard, Pame L. Romano, Mia Sai, D. F. Sanders, Dennis Shipman, Rick Sterling, Christopher S. Tourtellot, Loretta J. Walter, Karen Yue.

A special thank you to Reverend Carol Morishige, who in the final edits found the true essence of staying centered in love. Know that you made the difference.

Lastly, to my wife, Patti, who has been a partner in my life for more than 30 years. I believe together we have finally made sense of our magical lives. Your trust and guidance now come to light.

The Revised Edition Team: Lance Agena, David Bower, Sylvia D'Andrea, Lori RRossana Domingo, Stacie T. Lau, Larry Little, Kate Marciniak, Barbara Miyashiro, Karen Karinna Nielsen, Kendra Robinson-Harding, Patti Athenna Sterling, Rebecca Whitecotton.

Aloha,
Kahu Fred Sterling

Publisher's Preface

You are holding in your hands a copy of the Revised Edition of *Kirael: The Great Shift*. If you are fortunate to have one of the few copies of the original *Kirael: The Great Shift*, cherish it; it is no longer in print. Whether you are reading this material for the first time or the seventh, in this version you will find a few revisions of the original material and a more comprehensive glossary. You will also enjoy some new additions: a new introduction, updates at the beginning of each chapter, and more on Kirael and Kahu Fred Sterling. (*Kahu* means Spiritual Leader in Hawaiian.)

Kirael: The Great Shift was first published in early 1998, when few people were speaking of the shift in consciousness. The material for this book originated in the mid 1990s, during channeling sessions with Fred Sterling and a handful of Truth seekers wishing to develop their psychic abilities. It soon became evident that the information from Kirael was powerful and life changing. They knew that Kirael's words had to be shared with the world. As a result, this small group set out to transcribe the recorded sessions with Kirael and organize the material into a book. Their commitment to their own personal awakening through the collective effort was a grassroots self-publishing success—*Kirael: The Great Shift*.

No one would have imagined that what began as a few channeling sessions in private homes would grow into a worldwide spiritual healing entity. Initially called the Inward Healing Center, it has evolved into the Honolulu Church of Light, with its own healing programs, website and web broadcast, and in-house publishing company. All who are part of the organization have become healers, and some have chosen to become mediums and teachers. Each is dedicated to sharing the healing messages of Kirael and Fred Sterling with the world.

Kirael: The Great Shift contains the basics that everyone needs to know about the shift in consciousness that is awakening the planet. You are part of that awakening, and this book tells you that *you are not alone*. Many people who thought that they, alone, were experiencing seemingly inexplicable changes in their lives are now ready to speak out and ask questions that Kirael answers in this and other books. Kirael and Fred Sterling continue to speak out passionately about the Great Shift.

The good news is that you now find more people in the forefront of the spiritual awakening who, like Fred Sterling, are channeling messages about the shift in consciousness. This is in perfect alignment with recent planetary shifts: the 1987 Harmonic Convergence, the year 2000 millennial marker, the 2003 Harmonic Concordance, and the 2004 Venus transit. To be sure, you can now find more channeled information available today on the inter-connectedness of Earth shifts and spiritual awakening on a global level.

The other good news is that since the humble beginnings that brought forth *Kirael: The Great Shift*, there has been a steady stream of Kirael's wisdom available in print and audio recordings. For example, what Kirael references in this book as techniques for spiritual growth—Meditation, Sleepstate Programming, and Masterminding—are now incorporated into *Kirael: The Ten Principles of Consciously Creating* book and audio recordings.

Kirael: The Great Shift is a guidebook for an unprecedented event taking place on this planet, in *our* lifetime. The guides and messengers are here; the signposts are evident. It is about a journey of awakening, from fear into Love. We invite you to choose Love.

Aloha and Blessings,

Lightways Publishing
Honolulu, Hawaii

Preface and Introductions By the Author

Preface

What you hold in your hand is what I refer to as a "healing entity," for it will invoke thought, it will answer your questions, and it will expand the possibilities of your reality. Most of all, it will challenge each of you to move inward and search deeper, more than ever before. It will allow the heart to resonate with the vibration of Truth, Trust and Passion.

My life journey, from the depths of confusion to living by the principles of Truth, Trust and Passion, has been an awakening to the Great Shift in consciousness. Many of my dreams are being fulfilled as we make a difference in healing Mother Earth and humanity. The possibilities are unlimited as each of us chooses to heal in love.

If your heart resonates with any expression in this work, please tell someone about it, and if the need arises, be willing to pass it on. However, you may want to make it a loan, for this work is meant to be read many times. You will find that as your search expands so will the meaning of the passages.

Take the journey, test the work, and most of all awaken the inner source that has compelled you to pick up this vibration. Let the love flow and read with your heart. My heart, like this work, is open. TRUST.

New Introduction

Seven years ago, when this book was first published, we had a vision laid before us by Master Kirael that we knew we had to share with the world. Today, that vision has been embraced by many and echoed by other teachers in other metaphysical venues.

When this book was being written I was but a seeker looking to understand the meaning of the words that had come through me and were compiled into this work. Like so many, I asked the obvious questions: Was this the end time, or were we experiencing some sort of mystical unfolding of events that were shaping our future with seemingly no rhyme nor reason? Was there really something positive that could come from this incredibly startling energy now being called the Great Shift, and would it likely take all of our shared "realities" and teachings and shred them into some strange new way of life?

Maybe the most important question was how this little work was going to challenge the masses of information that seemed laced with negativity, doom and gloom, and aid We the People into knowing that we hold the key. Who was I to even think that my bringing Master Kirael to this plane would one day have answers that could benefit all?

Well, my friends, I have worked through the questions, and I now know that it is true. We are, as you hold this book in your hands, already immersed deeply into one of the most auspicious events to bless and alter our psyche since Master Jesus tried to help us heal back into love some 2000 years ago. It is a time of great awakening, and We the People are the stars in this cosmic adventure.

Master Kirael said at the time of this writing that seven levels of consciousness were embedded within the book, and that what was scribed on the pages was to be seen as timeless. No truer words have I heard coming from this Light Being. Readers have told me time and time again of the new information they find each time they read it. People who own the hard copy of this work have in many cases literally worn it out. In one case I was doing a book signing and a woman stepped in front of me with her book literally in pieces. In my heart I was so touched that I offered to trade her for a new signed copy at no cost. In a most stately manner she told me that nothing could make her part with her well-loved copy, and then she asked if I would be so kind as to sign it for her. In her words, she was just beginning to fully understand it and was truly satisfied exactly the way it was.

I am not a dreamer, my friends. In fact, I am always one of my own harshest critics. I say to each who will embark on the great awakening journey: there is so much to be learned from Master Kirael's interpretation of this awesome awakening. You need only look within your heart to test the truth of Master Kirael's words to know that what he speaks of is not a dream — it is a beautiful reality that we have the opportunity to create together.

There is a time where we must put our learned fears behind us and question the status quo. As well, there is a time when we must consider that as humans we do not have all the answers. Within the covers of this work, you will see a world unfold that not only gives us hope and courage, but also will help one begin to look forward to a space in time where we collectively can come together. No skin color, shape of eyes or personal history can stop us from uniting in a force that will move us to the next level of wakefulness.

As you read these words, trust that you have been led to a book written several years ago that makes even more sense to modern humankind than it did when it was first printed. The "why" is simple! We are already in this Great Shift. You cannot be awake in this world and not see the forces at work. You cannot use any of the five senses and not feel the pull of a sixth. It is a great time, my friends. It is "The Great Shift" and I am honored that you would be courageous enough to know that together we can ease this transformation of consciousness. Let's go together.

Let us open our hearts to the knowing that we must all participate. Let us not get stuck on the date of this awesome event. Rather, let us instead focus our energy of love on the outcome that we would all like to see. Let us prepare to awaken one day and find that peace has claimed this world. It must be our journey together, so let's climb the mountain as one.

Original Introduction

When this work began to unfold, I became its strongest critic. The potential of the material seemed to be beyond my comprehension. With only ten years of experience in the field, my level of exposure could be considered limited. Was it too soon to bring this exciting event of history to light, or should I continue to play in the safety of my own backyard? I struggled with this question, but I soon realized that bringing this work to light now would only have a positive effect in helping humankind understand the journey of life.

At this point, I was faced with my next challenge—how to allow Kirael free reign in this project, yet produce a work which will find its way into the hands of every single human who has become consciously aware of the following changes in our world and in our own individual journeys.

The state of the world today has many of us questioning our lives, our future, and our very existence. Often the information that we receive in the media creates an information overload that can result in confusion and chaos. Receiving information is essential in our lives, but much of what we receive only reveals the turbulent world we live in. It is at this time that we must learn to trust our inner feelings and guidance, for only then can we determine the need to explore our inward journey.

Many seem guided to slow down and understand what is important to them. Do you wonder why you have been drawn to this book, and why you are questioning your own curiosity? *Guidance has brought you here, my friends, and the journey is meant to create a space where the evolutionary journey may gain enlightenment.*

So, let's first attempt to clarify the term "guidance." Where does it come from and how does one tap into it? How do you tell the difference between your own complex thoughts, intuition and inner knowing, and outside influences? These are not simple questions, yet it is my personal belief that unless we can arrive at some level of clarity and understanding, the depth of this work will not be realized.

When I first submitted the transcripts to Oughten House Publications for direction, it became passionately clear that the information contained in it was guided to be shared with the general population. The material needed to be presented in such a way that the so-called "mainstream" reader would be able to accept it and share it with friends.

Much of my work is seen as "on the other side of acceptable" by average people, who are simply trying to get up every morning, go to work, and get by in today's mainstream society. Somehow, if the pretense is vivid enough, all of the turmoil in their lives will magically disappear.

Like myself not so long ago, many people are not ready to challenge their beliefs about the world as they perceive it. There is safety in staying within the mass belief system. Being part of the majority lends false courage, and this is where the real problem lies. It is in the best interests of the so-called "powers at large" to maintain this mass illusion. They depend on the fear embedded in the mass illusion to maintain their control, and the material in this book clearly will not meet with their approval.

I am not trying to invoke some sort of grand conspiracy theory, for all Kirael has put forth in this work are possibilities for each reader to ponder. Writing this book has opened up my own belief system beyond my wildest expectations. So indulge with me in a few more paragraphs, while I explain where this all came from. It is from the desire of all those beautiful spirits who wish to be of loving guidance to humankind.

The human journey is one that each individual experiences differently. Few are even consciously aware of the deep meaning of what is called the human experience. This is a book of guidance for all to use on their own spiritual journeys.

There is a reason why you have chosen this day to take the time to pick up this book. It is no coincidence. These words are not intended for any specific type of person but are meant to be shared with all who choose to listen with an open heart. If your hands are touching this book, if your eyes are reading these words, if your heart is skipping, and you feel a warmth surround you, know that your inner spirit is reawakening. As all of us search for more love and light within our lives, it is important to recognize this opportunity for growth and welcome it.

Please remember to read these words with a loving heart and open mind. Although consciously you may not understand some of the material, know that somewhere in the depths of your subconscious mind, your memory is reawakening. And through this reawakening, your current life will flow with more love, clarity, abundance, and understanding than ever before.

It is an honor and a privilege to be at a point in life to begin to understand the value of this information. The words of this book have brought tremendous clarity to my present level of consciousness. I hope you will join me as this magical journey from fear to love unfolds, and we can begin the healing.

My Introduction to Kirael

Back in the late 1980s, my wife dragged me kicking and screaming to a series of metaphysical workshops. The reason for my resistance was quite simple: my belief system was based on my attachments to the five senses. If I could touch it, see it, feel it, or somehow fit it into the reality of my five senses, I felt comfortable. So to me these workshops were what I referred to as "weird." I found myself participating in the ancient practice of table tapping, getting answers from a stone suspended from a string, and observing the art of trance mediumship.

After allowing the original uneasiness to pass, I went immediately from "I can't believe this is happening" to an overwhelming desire to experience more. I was intrigued by the trance channeling sessions and captivated by the information coming from a source outside of my current reality.

One afternoon while sitting through a session, I started dozing off. After a time I opened my eyes and everyone in the room was staring at me with the strangest expressions. Fortunately, there was a tape recorder in the room, which provided evidence that I had suddenly and unexpectedly entered the world of mediumship.

This was my first experience of being a trance medium for a higher being or vibrational energy pattern from another dimensional reality. The entity, who had a pronounced Scottish-sounding accent, asked that we refer to him as "Kirael." As Kirael familiarized himself with the physical world of the Third Dimension, we very quickly became used to each other. Such was the beginning of a long and wondrous relationship that has been of service to many who are searching for answers not readily available to people on this Earth plane.

Over the years, I have heard all the rational explanations about what trance channeling is—from split personality to possession. Some people need to make sense of this phenomenon by defining it through their linear thinking. However, I believe one must move past the limitations of our physical reality to fully appreciate the experience. The information coming forth from Kirael about historical and future events resonates on a higher vibration than would ordinarily be possible due to the density of the Third Dimension.

Kirael has always maintained that when one is truly ready to meet him, the opportunity will present itself. You are invited to call upon Kirael as you read this book to bring forth this light energy and allow the healing to begin. Whenever you call on his energy, Kirael will be with you.

So let your higher consciousness guide this life time. Experience the pure love of an entity from another dimension who has purposefully revealed The Great Shift to be not a horrendous upheaval, but a thing of wonderment and excitement, which will give all a new hope. The world is ready to heal. Let us begin together.

—Kahu Fred Sterling

Prologue

KIRAEL: I would like to thank all of We the People that so honor the work that I brought onto this Earth plane. When we first brought this book out so many years ago, we told the world of this Great Shift, the Great Shift in Consciousness, and the world, for the most part, truly wasn't ready to hear it. Yet, every book we had, we sold.

So it was something that was lying deep within each soul. It was a cellular consciousness, a knowingness, that something was about to happen and nobody knew what it was. I spent the greater part of those years trying to tell the people when they'd ask me this question: When is this Great Shift, Master Kirael? And I would say to them this: The Great Shift is happening even as you ask me, for the Great Shift is about We the People of planet Earth awakening to a new vibration of existence. It is about We the People seeing things that they have never seen before, experiences they have never had before. The Great Shift is about the awakening of the fullness of your love and connection with the great Creator's Force.

It is where We the People will begin to raise their vibration. They will walk hand in hand in harmonious peace. They will love one another on another level that has not been seen since the time of Lemuria. There will be those who'll read this and not even know that Lemuria existed. But I tell you this: Each and every one of you who reads this for the first time, you're living on a planet that is so loved by the God Creator, so honored by those of us in spirit, that we have come in great collective force to be a party to your great excursion.

We don't think about dates because we know, as we are writing this today, that we are already in the Great Shift. Systems that you have seen for years that seemed to be so solid now seem very weakened, don't they? The great things with religions, the great things with politics, the great belief systems that we refer to as the matrix—all of that is breaking at the edges now.

Oh, it's not going to disappear overnight, because you are not ready. Even we in the Guidance Realm could be considered not ready. But we are working hard for you. We are trying everything we can to make ourselves heard in your heart. Some of the greatest beings have come to your Earth plane in service now. Brothers and sisters of light giving up their existence within the Creator that they may walk upon the Earth with you, great beings that have actually come into embodiment—many of them will be drawn to this book. Maybe it is you who I am speaking to.

But know this: There are no surprises in the Great Shift. It is a time for great awakening. It is a time to feel the presence of love again. It is a time for peace to prevail on your Earth plane. And this is what we hope, this is what we pray, this is what we cause our thoughts to collect to do. We pray that each and every person who reads this book will be touched on a very deep level, that they don't need to shout from the rooftops. They need to focus within themselves and find the love.

I've heard stories that the original version of this book was passed from one to the next, and then I hear from the same people their tears of crying because they don't have the book anymore. This is not a book, my friends, that you read once and cast to grow dust in the corner. This is a book written in such fashion by a master guide that it is meant for you to read over and over, and that each time you read it, each time it will take you deeper and deeper into your heart.

Me medium's editors have been reading it to make sure it is proper for you, and I've watched them cry page after page—not from sadness, my friends, but from the pure enjoyment of knowing that there is hope, that it is not a lost cause. Can you ask more from a work than that?

So it is in me heart that I open to you today that you will read me work with the openness that me editors have done, and you will let it touch you, let it play with the strings of your heart. And if a wee tear falls upon your cheek, bless yourself but feel not bad. Know that this book is written from the highest amount of love that could be brought forth.

I would suggest that as you read it, you sit calmly, quietly. Put just the right light on. Maybe turn on a little bit of music softly behind you, and tell everyone else in the house: do not disturb. For this is the way you will enjoy this work time and time again.

The Great Shift, my friends, do not look for it. Don't try to figure out when it is going to happen. It's on you now. And some of you are already falling in love with it, aren't you? For those of you that aren't, just bear with it. What you see is the bumpy road. It is me solemn vow that if you stand with some of the things you'll read in this work, the bumps in the road will smooth out. This I know because this I have already witnessed.

·1·

Welcome to the Great Shift!

UPDATE FROM KIRAEL

KIRAEL: The Great Shift. So many were wondering what it was, when it was going to happen, who was going to participate, only to find out that there is only one participant. One participant. And that is you reading these words—every one of you, because one day you come to understand there is only one.

And so I say to each and every one that reads this particular part of the work, that the Great Shift is the upliftment from one level of consciousness to the next. It is the awakening of parts of your brain, parts of your cellular consciousness, that have never been awake before, for there was no reason for them to be awake. It was a time of the great matrix. It was a time when you let a few decide for you.

But no longer will it be, my friends. This is the Great Shift in Consciousness. This is the one where We the People arise in love and in the truth of a peace without violence. It is a time, my friends, when the Earth plane will shift to a new level of consciousness. I say it this way: Most of you would agree reading this that you are in what you call the third dimension. It is a dimension based in duality. It is a dimension based in the yin and yang. Everything has opposites.

But you are going to a place, my friends, I used to be able to say slowly but surely, but not anymore. You are going to a place where you will come to find out that truth is something that you never anticipated it to be. You are going to a place where you will differentiate the difference between passion and raw excitement. You are going to a place where clarity will reign in everything that you see. You will know how to communicate on levels you never thought possible.

There are many of you already beginning to be able to see in one's eyes the truth of what I am speaking about. But most important, my friends, the Great Shift means that you can be in love, pure love, and not have to think that you might be just a little bit strange because of it.

And lastly about your Great Shift, we're there with you. Oh, you'll hear from us in all different sorts and names and ways, but we're there with you. The Creator has sent us on our best light ever. What a thrill we find here, watching a whole civilization. Where in the past the great beautiful Creator has had to lift all of you from the Earth plane in order to reset and get Mother Earth pure in light again, this time your Creator has so much confidence in its own Light, me and you, that he wants you to stay aboard the planet.

You will read in the rest of this chapter that there is nothing to fear. You get to stay aboard to lift Mother Earth through the most beautiful experience she'll ever have. What a grand way to go. God bless.

•••

KIRAEL: It's a time of great excitement! It's a time to begin a wondrous journey into the reawakening of your Truth essence. It's a time to release fear and embrace freedom. But what is freedom? Simple. It's the recognition that you came to Earth on a mission, a mission to experience everything that the Third Dimension has to offer. As the duration of the Third Dimension comes swiftly to an end, there are rumors of a Great Shift that will permeate every aspect of your Earth plane. Earth changes are imminent. Almost all views that you currently hold will need adjustment. A shift in consciousness has begun that is so great that it will be recognized as the greatest event in humanity's history. So be excited, my friends, and journey with us as we unfold the possibilities of self-empowerment, a return to wholeness, and fulfillment of your highest potential.

I want everyone to know that it doesn't matter if you are just beginning your journey or have attained a high spiritual evolution. This book holds Truths for all. Often the difference between what you hear and the way you feel is vast. It's not so much what you "hear" when you read these words, but what you feel. Some of the words you will read here may have a number of meanings, and the material may challenge your current belief systems.

Some may feel this is the end of the world. However, let me assure you that Mother Earth will be here for a long time to come, though maybe not as you recognize Her today. This Shift, which brings some of the most beautiful conscious awareness that has ever been experienced, is already upon you as you read this book. So it might be said that *the world as you recognize it today* is coming to an end, only to be replaced by a world that is beyond your wildest expectations.

This new world will offer completely new experiences, such as communicating without the voice, traveling without the physical body, and experiencing love without fear. The truth of the words "brothers and sisters" will become a reality. Powerful governments, world orders, chaos, and wars will become a thing of the past. So live in fear if you must, but this work is meant to take you beyond all that. It is meant to be a wellspring of information that will show you how to resonate with this new energy. It is a guidebook to make your journey the most powerful experience you have ever encountered in any of your lifetimes.

You have lived multiple lives on your evolutionary journey. Not one of your past lives has been time wasted, as you chose to experience everything possible. This journey called the Third Dimension is coming to an abrupt end as we move into the evolutionary possibilities of the Fourth Dimension. If it has been your choice to feel out of control and absorbed by the fast pace of the Earth plane, then I simply ask that you empower yourself. Make a new choice. Release the fear, embrace the beauty, and love everything this new journey offers. This book will show you how, and will open the gate for you to empower yourself.

For thousands of years, you have been on a journey of self-discovery. This journey has brought you all the way through the Third Dimension. Now the journey is moving you into an all-new experience, a new era. That is why it is called a "new age."

Since the dawn of humanity, there has been a constant fear that you might lose your way returning to the Creator. Fear has been used to prevent you from skipping ahead in the journey. This has worked for millennia, but fear can no longer be used to minimize the acceleration of the journey. In simplest form, you can no longer use the pretense of "I don't know" because, as the knowing awakens, my friends, you will move into enjoying this journey 100 percent.

Please remember that evolution is based on the journey, so throughout this book I emphasize totally enjoying the journey. The outcome of all linear thought patterns is pre-manifested and is awaiting the prescribed time to manifest from the Fourth Dimension to the Third. Please be crystal clear that every action taken by human consciousness is, in fact, a choice. Each choice you make creates a pathway to a new journey. Choose carefully, for if you have a thought, it is only a matter of time before it will manifest in your reality.

I have come here to share with you many new and sometimes difficult ideas that may at times stretch your belief systems. One thing you may rely on is that I will always speak from Truth. I may not always say what you want to hear, yet I can guarantee that what I say is what you *need* to hear. It is with great resolution that I am guided to follow the path of the Christ Energy in these teachings of Love and Healing.

I am most assuredly not here to become your teacher or to sway your thinking to any single belief system. My intent is to offer many different potentials as to how you may not only get through this Shift, but moreover, how to prepare, and yes, even enjoy your part in it. As you ponder over the possibilities, keep the following foremost in your mind:

> Hold onto and enjoy the parts you like, and for those you don't like, simply put them on the side, for at their own pace, each will bring *itself forward.*

Shifts Recognized by Historical Fact

Approximately every 2,000 years, the Earth plane undergoes a shift. About 7,000 to 8,000 years ago, the Creator unveiled a plan that allowed for a more thorough journey so that all of you could expand and return to the Creator. By reincarnating in the Earth plane, you have forfeited the luxury, so to speak, of living in the so-called higher experiences. I say "so-called" because it is truly an honor bestowed on the Self, by the Self, to be able to experience this journey called the Third Dimension. It is clear that the only separation that truly exists between an Earth-bound entity (human) and the Creator Essence is a veil of awareness, and the history of human existence has been an evolutionary process of raising your vibration so that you can move through this veil with grace and beauty.

Approximately 6,000 years ago, the period referred to as the "Egyptian Pharaohs" lasted about 2,000 years, until Moses began to unify his followers. This period was marked by great turmoil up to and throughout the receiving of the Ten Commandments. The unfolding events culminated in a new freedom of thought over the next 2,000 years until, as history shows, the Master Jesus brought forth a new reality onto the Earth plane. Again, great turmoil seemed to have infused the evolutionary plan. Notice that each period lasted approximately 2,000 years. Is not the similarity between the events around the lifetime of Jesus and where we are now striking?

The New Age

The New Age actually took place 2,000 years ago when the Christ Consciousness permeated evolution. One of the reasons people dislike the term "new age" today is because, in reality, the Shift was intended to have taken place then. Though consciously unaware of it, most were anticipating an even larger Shift than what actually took place. This created a sense of unfulfillment. To this day, those same evolving souls still dislike the term "new age." However, I can assure you, my friends, that you will not be disappointed this time around.

The End of Time

In reality, time as you recognize it is an illusion, but one that is losing its power. As a result, time is becoming compressed. Now, you are the Creator's Energy that was sent off as a formatted thought, only to evolve back to love. In this evolutionary process, you were given only so many thousands of years to actually play out your journey in the Third Dimension and to go through all the possibilities of experience. You are then expected to return in complete fullness to the Creator. This is why you must now complete the experiences of the Third Dimension and prepare to enter the enlightenment of the Fourth Dimension. This is why it is so important to use the remaining time to complete the experiences of the Third Dimension and not waste any of the beautiful essence of the Fourth Dimension.

As most are aware, it is the Creator's Will that all living essence must move towards its final completion through what is known as "evolution." In this oftentimes chaotic process, the Earth, like all other living entities, must also fulfill Her own destiny. The time and space of Earth in the Third Dimension is quickly coming to an end. Therefore, anything vibrating at this level must transcend to new heights in order to function within the new essence. Hence, the journey from the Third Dimension to the Fourth.

Big Changes Ahead

A phenomenon known as the "Photon Energy" will come into contact with Earth soon after the turn of the century, but the date is most difficult to actually pinpoint. With the awakening of the population, Mother Earth will make the final decision. You see, Her speed and total knowing are factors in the actual timing. The more awake you become, the greater the passion to complete your experiences as quickly as possible. Please believe me when I say that time is not on your side. Awaken, my friends. Awaken!

You might think that the coming changes will be excessive, depending on your level of evolution at the time of this Shift. Mother Earth will most definitely make some adjustments. For instance, your scientific community is well aware that the planet's magnetic poles have already begun to shift and that Her rotational speed is changing. In addition, Her land masses are shifting, causing a great deal of compression. The Earth's plates are moving together and rolling on top of each other, causing more than a hundred earthquakes a day, some detectable and some not. Common sense alone tells you that the landmass configurations are changing.

Earth's atmospheric pressure is increasing because of the erosion of the ozone layers caused by humankind's mishandling of Mother Earth's resources. In addition, the influences from the Photon Energy are also beginning to compress the Earth's surface. The Photon Energy vibrates at a very different rate than you are accustomed to and contributes to the alarming sense of time speeding up.

There is no question about it: Mother Earth is compressing and shifting, and along with it, everything else (including time) must compress and shift, too. Even your human bodies are shifting. That's why you feel the pressure on your physical body. The pressure that's being applied to Mother Earth right now and Her efforts to adjust to those pressures are causing this compression factor.

Let us speak for a moment of the islands of Hawaii. These islands are, in fact, mountaintops of the ancient continent of Lemuria. You may not have heard of this, as recorded history begins after the age of Atlantis. Yet, my friends, there is a lot more history which will soon be revealed as the information within the chambers of the Great Pyramid is made available to the world. In the upheaval of the Earth changes, the Hawaiian Islands will actually gain landmass, whereas other parts of the world may actually lose their current formation. It is not my desire to cause panic but to support all to seek their own level of preparation for the Shift.

On the subject of chaos, it is not my intent to scare you but to enlighten, for chaos is in fact part of the Shift. You will not have to wait for chaos because you have already begun to experience this in a minor fashion. For instance, television exposes you to horrendous events that are only a prelude of things to come. Reading this book will help you avoid becoming part of the chaos. With knowledge and a true understanding of the process, you will not only get through the Shift, but you will find a clarity that helps smooth the way.

The Creator has a divine plan that embraces all of those who can come to the realization of unity. Many will choose the ways of the old and attempt to push and shove their way into the new era. This will not work. The more you understand cooperation through love and healing, the quicker your clarity will focus on assisting one another. Through this process, many more will evolve into the new age.

Now let us look at this from the perspective of Mother Earth. In your lengthy quest of discovery, you have disrupted Her reality with such unthinkable acts as cutting Her beautiful forests, disposing of poisonous waste in Her once pure waterways, and releasing horrible, toxic gases into what once were Her pristine blue skies. Do you believe that this outrage could have gone on much longer without divine intervention?

So all these things will come to pass; there is no question about it. Please be clear: All that I have said so far, and more, will come to pass, yet it is not the intent of the Creator to end your civilization, but rather to bring you the opportunity of beauty, tranquility, and loving grace. Read on with zest. What is to be revealed shall only enhance your journey, for those who are reading this book are the very ones who will be charged with assisting the evolution of beautiful Mother Earth.

There are soothsayers holding signs saying "The End of the World Is Coming," but it will not happen that way. The Great Shift, my friends, is not the end of the world. Let's be very clear about that. However, the world as you recognize it is going to end. The Shift is not coming, my friends; it is not coming at all. *It is already here.* The

Shift is with you as we speak. Be clear on this. The Shift is not coming! The Shift is here! You are already in the Great Shift!

Galactic Brotherhood

You may have heard of the "Galactic Brotherhood." They are often referred to as extra-terrestrials, space beings, and many other names. Please do not see them as a threat. In fact, they are most peaceful and non-threatening, for they have chosen to assist humanity through the Shift.

The Hubble Space Telescope has revealed that the Milky Way galaxy—the one you live in—has 100 billion suns with planetary systems just like yours. And your galaxy is but one of 200 billion galaxies in the universe. Think about it! 200 billion galaxies with 100 billion suns per galaxy. Hello! Do you still think you might be the only ones out there? To believe you are would be total arrogance. Does it make sense that the Creator with all Its glorious power would create one planet in 200 billion galaxies that has the only life forms in existence? If I could figure out how to laugh in print, I would do it here!

For those of you who struggle with this concept, let me reveal that I'm not from your Earth plane. I'm not even from your galaxy. In reality, I come from the Seventh Dimension, whereas you live in the Third. The next dimension, the Fourth, is the dimension of thought. Next, the Fifth is a realm where no duality (yin and yang) exists, the dimension of pure love. Then we go on to the Sixth, Seventh, and so on, which I will describe in future books.

Throughout this book, I refer to many of the civilizations within the Galactic Brotherhood, such as the Sirians, Pleiadians, and Andromedans. Each has had its influence on your Earth plane, and each has a stake in the outcome of your post-Shift reality. There are those among you who believe that the Galactic Brotherhood is separate from the Earth consciousness. Let me make it abundantly clear: they are not coming—they are already here! Due to their exceptional technology, they can exist within your atmosphere without detection. (I will talk more about this in Chapter 6.)

Three Days of Darkness: Don't Panic!

One of the processes of the Shift is the entry into the Photon Energy through its outer edge, the Belt. This transition has been termed the "Three Days of Darkness." During this period, the Earth plane will undergo a darkness that you have never experienced before. As an example, during the three days of darkness, if you were to hold your hand a few inches in front of your eyes, you would not be able to see it. This darkness is most difficult to describe, for it has never happened before. My friends, this is a time when you will need to stay centered, for this is a time when fear will loom largest. However, by the time you have read more about this in Chapter 8, you will feel confident and almost look forward to this particular time.

When the darkness happens and temperatures begin to drop, you may be concerned about family members who have little awareness of what's happening. Simply know that each soul, acting as an individual, has chosen its path home. If your loved ones are lagging behind in their awareness, then I can only say, "Try your best." Those souls, seemingly unconcerned with what's happening on the Earth at this time, are only a blink away from understanding. Just let them hear your version. It's not about completely changing the way they believe, but about simply planting the seeds of knowledge and trusting the Creator to bring them along far enough to see the need for awakening.

Three Choices to the Shift

There are three ways in which you may experience the Great Shift. Firstly, you may choose to "return home"—some refer to this as dying—where you will return to your origins and have no further contact with the Earth plane. Secondly, you may move to the so-called "holographic world" (covered in a future book). And thirdly, you can choose "evolution," meaning simply the desire and the ability to move from the Third Dimension into the Fourth, or the process known as "ascension."

Let me assure you that if you have read this far, it is most likely you have already chosen ascension. Welcome to the Shift!

The Importance of Experience

Through beauty, great love, and the ability to focus, the Creator brought the Earth plane into existence, and human existence began in what has been referred to as the "schoolhouse of creative evolution." This existence, in truth, was simply a thought that took on life as you know it today, for thought is the beautiful journey that allows the wonders of experience. The Creator's focus of energy was brought in to support human experience, so we must be clear that no failure has taken place. In truth, evolution is in its divine order.

Avoid the tendency to use the Great Shift as an excuse to shrug off the experience. For instance, why sign a long-term contract when the possibilities exist that soon after the turn of the century, the new era will be upon us? This, my friends, would be a grave mistake because it would negate what you are learning in your current journey. I must emphasize: *Those who take shortcuts will surely have to deal with the results post-Shift.*

You cannot shortcut this thing, my friends. If you are looking to sign a 30-year mortgage, go ahead and sign it. Something that is needed in your soul's evolution should always be followed for its learning possibilities. Maybe it is part of your plan to experience a long-term debt, and using the Shift as an excuse to put it off will only serve as a setback in your particular journey.

Another example might be the purchase of a new automobile. You may ask, "Why should I buy it? If in fact there will be no fossil fuel after the Shift, why should I waste my money?" If it were not in the plan for you to experience this, the subject would never have presented itself.

A last example before we move on. You might say to yourself, "Why should I continue to make all these monthly payments if what Kirael is saying is true? After all, when the Shift is complete, there will be no real need for our current money exchange system. So why should I continue?" It's easy, my friends. Where do you suppose you might find it in the Creator's plan that you should not meet your obligations? Nowhere, my friends. Common sense says that the one thing not needed in the new journey is a bunch of incomplete karmic issues, so please make sure they are completed on this side.

In simple terms, you have a few remaining years to go through and heal your lower vibrational experiences. Please do not waste this opportunity. Learn with diligence and prepare to enter the Fourth Journey in the highest of lights, carrying as little baggage as possible. Living your life "in the now" assures you of experiencing all with completeness.

Remember, you planned a full set of experiences over a prescribed period of time upon entering the Earth plane on your current journey. It was known at the time that you would experience the Shift, yet that had little influence on the fullness of your plan. So you will assure yourself of success only by completing the current experience in its entirety.

Just as a very simple example, let's suppose you are on your fourth spouse in this lifetime. Just possibly in the last lifetime, you were harmoniously married to one individual, and you lived that whole lifetime in a single-mate situation. When you planned your return to Earth, you decided to experience multiple spouses, so you have three, four, five marriages. Others may say, "Oh, you've really wrecked this life because you've had four or five marriages." That's not wrecking your life. For your own purposes, you needed to experience four or five different marriages in the same lifetime.

So you see, everything is evolution. I know some of you will struggle with this, especially my scientific friends. They like to put A and B together, divide it by seven and multiply by two. It does not always work that simply. The truth is that you have been here on Earth a number of times, and you will be here a number of times more, each time with a plan.

There was a time when you had the luxury of continually repeating your lessons. However, the time compression of the Earth plane is creating an acceleration of your experiences. This means you will be experiencing multiple lessons simultaneously in your life. In the past, your higher self had little reason to hurry because all evolving souls had many lifetimes to explore their experiences. This, of course, is no longer possible because the Third Dimension is rapidly coming to a close.

As each soul established its journey on Earth, it could give itself ample room for long, drawn out, repetitive experiences, and even decide to switch to new experiences, knowing it could complete certain projects in future lives. For instance, this book was to have been written some time ago. All the people currently involved in the project had the opportunity to complete the task in other lifetimes. Many of them began the project and, at some point, it seemed insurmountable. It was put off for one reason or another, but now all those individuals have been brought back together to complete the project. Of course, their mission has expanded from just this one book to a series of books, since that is what it will take to prepare humanity for this Shift.

Resistance

Many people will begin to recognize this compression of experience and, as in the past, they will want to say, "I can't make it." I will share with you why that won't work this time.

Those of you evolving on this new journey must be as free as possible of the old experiences. No one wants to use precious time rehashing old programs while the rest are moving forward at such a phenomenal pace, like being held back in school while your friends move on. They are still your friends, but nothing is ever really the same.

There are those who will complain that it seems to get worse every day. I say to you, first of all, change your thinking. Don't join the consensus mindset permeating the Earth plane. Each must begin to focus on what can be done as opposed to what seems impossible.

Not only is help available, it is now so close to your conscious awareness that all you have to do is ask during prayer and listen during meditation. Most of you are already aware of how fast thoughts are manifesting. Simply look at everything happening in your life, and experience all that you possibly can in this time.

The Importance of Meditation

Nobody will escape the Great Shift because it is in the Creator's plan of evolution. In truth, it is already here! It will be accompanied by the Photon Energy (see Chapter 4), whose effects we are already experiencing. The whole Earth plane will resonate with it soon after the turn of the century. Those who will remain on Earth must begin now to prepare their body systems for ascension.

What guidance can be offered to help make this process without not only fear but also exciting? Begin by mastering the basics such as meditation, meditation, and meditation. Let me assure you that this is not a typographical error. Through the simplicity of meditation, you realize the true inner force you possess to attune to the higher vibrational realities. Without this ability, you will find yourself becoming aligned with the chaos permeating Mother Earth.

You must maintain clarity of thought because most will find themselves overrun with fear. As I have stated before, this is the one thing that must be avoided, for fear will block the path of evolution. Be reminded that we are not talking about the end of the world, although some of the changes will be major. You must be ready to see the beauty that has been laid out in the Shift.

Meditation is your foundation from here forward, my friends. Meditation is all there really is. It is the forum in which you can get in touch with your guides and higher self. Praying is the asking, and meditating is the listening that opens you to receive the answer—not just hearing, but listening, with clarity.

How meditation works is often misunderstood. Meditation is the one true connection between your four-body system. The connection starts with your physical body, which connects to your emotional body. From there, it proceeds to the mental body and completes the connection to the spiritual body. Each body plays a unique role in your growth, yet to evolve completely, you must learn the total connection of all our systems in oneness. It is through meditation that you truly begin to understand the meaning of life.

Preparing the Children

I talk now about the little ones, the ones born into the Earth dimension as we speak. They bring information with them. They are the ones who have come from home, so to speak. They have come to Earth to not only enjoy and be a part of the Shift but also to bring immense knowledge with them. Stop "goo-gooing" in their face and talk to them like real people. Then they will tell you what they know.

Like your dolphins, whales, and other high beings, they do not use a lot of words to get their message across. All you need to do is ask a small child, "So what do you want to tell us?" Then sit back and listen. You will be surprised at what they have to say. Those who are older, born around 1985, are going to have to get ready, just as the adult population must. The problem is that the adult population is not moving along very fast, so we on our side may have to "push" you, so to speak.

Do not worry about the children, my friends. They will come into this at a much more rapid rate because they have not had 30, 40, or 50 years to immerse themselves in the Third Dimension. They will come right into the Shift in fullness. The children have messages to be heard, and they can be quite forceful in how they deliver them. If you really want to get involved, simply ask these little ones to tell you where God is from and what the truth is. The answers you receive will astound you.

One evening during "An Evening with Kirael," a young person asked the following question: "Kirael, does God have a Mommy and Daddy? And if He does, they must be real proud of Him, right?" That is typical of the thought-provoking queries children are capable of asking. Simply learn to communicate with a younger person on a little higher level and you will come away with some real learning.

Congratulations to all who have chosen to become schoolteachers, because it is with this courage that the little ones are able to ascend.

You Are the Creator

I will now share a simple concept with you. Before time was measured, the Creator God looked on the creation called Earth and concluded that in all that beauty, one element had been overlooked. Even with all Its infinite wisdom, the Creator had no way to experience Its own totality. So, the Creator began to focus the entire power of Its thought on how this might be accomplished. In this focus, the human species was conceived. This Creator Essence would now experience Its own creation simply by veiling Itself from Its own identity. This, my friends, is how evolution began.

Since its creation, the human being has been journeying in its purest thought form, on one single path to become once again one with its Creator, for all eternity. Each of you is a product of this thought pattern.

Like the Creator Essence, with which you are one, you possess the ability of manifestation. Within this process, all may truly create reality by simply focusing with passion. Know that every thought sent into the etheric fabric assumes some sort of life form. Your clarity, intent, and passion determine what dimension it will manifest in as well as the time frame needed for it to become reality.

If you were to learn only one thing from this book, it would be that the power of manifesting is needed here and now. The ability to manifest is not something you need to learn. You were born into this space completely equipped to succeed. The only question is when you will begin to lift the self-imposed veil and allow your light body the freedom to experience the limitless possibilities.

Be assured, my friends, the journey has no completion, but only a new set of experiences to enjoy. Start now to explore the many paths of evolution, and remember that the ultimate goal is to return to the Creator's Essence with your Truth and Light.

·2·

Journey From Fear to Love

UPDATE FROM KIRAEL

KIRAEL: Ooh, I love this chapter. Really I do. And I'll tell you why.

The journey from fear to love is the experience of the Shift itself, for much of what you do in this Earth plane is done from fear. Don't most of you pay taxes because you are afraid of the tax man? Don't most of you do much of what you do in your job because you are afraid you are going to be fired? Don't many of you bring your children up afraid that you are going to fail? This is the journey, my friend, from fear to love.

If the fear has driven you to your knees on more than one occasion, celebrate that. You say, "Master Kirael, I should celebrate being driven to me knees?" Yes, you should be, because, you see, when you get driven to your knees, don't you know, that's where you start to do your prayers. Prayers not of some religious experience, but prayers of clarity, prayers communicated in the fullness of the journey.

Oh, yes. And then one day you begin to do this Great Shift, and you just say, "No more. No more fear." You say, "Master Kirael, can it be that easy?" Well, I've never professed anything to be that easy. I'll ask you: Do you think it would be worth the journey? Because, you see, if it is, that's what this chapter is all about. It's about the journey from fear to love.

It's about awakening one day, and saying to yourself, "I've got nothing to be afraid of because the Creator loves me." You wake up one day, and you say, "You know what I figured out? The Creator makes no mistakes. Therefore, everything in this life is just like they said in the past: it's perfect."

Some of you reading this, don't you know, you haven't gone to your knees yet, and you are still fighting everything you can and falling prey to the fears. But one day, after you have read it enough, you'll wake up. I promise you'll wake up from a sound sleep in the middle of night, and you will say, "Oh, my God, it is the Great Shift in Consciousness."

I say to each and every one who will read this: It is time that you release your fears, that you open your heart to the love that surrounds you. Oh, don't look for it in your partners in life; they are working just like you are. But go outside after you finish reading here today. Find yourself a beautiful tree, find yourself a flower, find yourself a bubbling brook, and you will know who loves you the most. Your Creator loves you, because it put all of this here for you.

And you drive past it every day lickety-split; you never see a thing. You just see the road before you, because you are afraid that you are going to be late to get where you are going. And when the red light turns red, your fingers drumming on that steering wheel, and you feel the frustration building in your chest, remember these words: the Creator doesn't make any mistakes. Nor do you.

Take a deep breath. Look on the corner over there where that pretty man or that pretty woman is. Look at the lady selling flowers. Look at the texture of the buildings around you. You say, "But Master Kirael, what if they are dirty?" That would be the fear talking. Imagine them clean and crisp and brand new. And imagine what you'd like the world to look like, and then you will have done the journey from fear to love. Do you get it?

●●●

KIRAEL: The vast majority of people here on Earth walk around in fear of loss. Somewhere, my friends, they began to learn about fear and grew away from love. The true fear is that, in essence, they may never find their way home to the Great Creator. In this fear, they build up many, many belief systems that deter their own growth. Healing will bring forth their ability to center themselves, to be relieved of fear and brought in ssence of love once again.

We're trying to assist people to understand that this healing is about clarity and about staying centered within themselves. It's about having to reach inside to check that the heart beats in purity and clarity. My friends, it is about conquering all those fears that are part of your life. It is about understanding that fear is self-imposed and that love is only, in reality, "a flip of the switch" away.

You may say, "Kirael, I don't want to take that kind of responsibility. I don't want to have to think positive all the time." I'm telling you, my friends, you'd better get straight with yourself. If you want the good things in your life, you have to start thinking of them now. You'd be so much happier if you didn't buy into negativity. At some point in this evolutionary journey, you will no longer be manipulated by fear. You will love yourself too much to let that happen. The key to your entire evolutionary journey, my friends, is love. Within love is the chance to find that inner peace that you seek.

The journey is filled with exciting aspects called "experiences." This allows evolution to become a natural part of every moment. Most people here in the Third Dimension are more concerned with arriving at a specific goal than what it will actually take to get there. I seldom refer to anything as an absolute, yet this will be one exception. Concentrating on the end result slows your growth because, in most cases, the end result is not what you figured it would be. The best way to begin to work past this is to become totally focused on what it is you want first. As soon as you are clear on this, simply begin the journey. You have only a limited span on Earth, so it makes perfect sense to spend every second wisely. Enjoy your journey!

Heal that inner spirit, the soul consciousness. When that becomes healed to the point where you understand and love fear for what it has to offer, you get closer and closer to having no fear. The more healed you become, the less you tolerate fear in your life. The quicker you heal, the quicker you understand the journey, which is a journey to love anyway.

In the essence of the Creator, the journey is nothing but love, pure love. Creation is based on love, but in order for you to experience the Third Dimension, the Creator allowed fear. All you need to do is choose to heal yourself of that fear, my friends, and you are in love.

Truth, Trust, Passion

The Trinity of Truth, Trust and Passion anchors the healing of love within the self. If you integrate the trinity into all facets of your life, the choices you make will move you into balance and fulfillment. It is the basis of love. Look at it as a three-legged stool: if one leg is shorter than the rest, the stool will not sit correctly. Shorten any one leg enough and the stool will topple. This is why we place so much emphasis on the Trinity.

Truth

Truth is the essence from which all reality extends. It is not just a word but the totality of understanding how life works. There are no such things as half-truths, shaded-truths, or one of the best, little white lies. I say this because when you begin to experience being in truth at all times, you will dislike the feeling of hearing untruth. How often have you told one lie, only to have to formulate others to cover it up? When you start down the path of total truth, believe me, there is no turning back.

One of the most important truths is self love, which means being true to yourself. You are usually being true to yourself because your essence is that of the Creator, which is unconditional love. In your society, you are taught to help and love others, but you are not taught to love yourself. If you would shower yourself with love, you would become so full of love that you would be able to share it with others. *The most important person to love is you.*

Everyone needs love. When you do not have self-love, you seek it elsewhere, oftentimes by substituting external things such as drugs and alcohol, and most often, by abusing self or others. When you accept total Truth in your life, it becomes evident that Truth is actually self-love.

Trust

In order to fully understand trust, you must realize the power of *knowing*, which comes from being in your truth. To align with trust, you must understand that it happens on a deeper level than you may be willing to experience. Trust is more than a word—it is a resonance. Whether in a personal relationship or a business deal, the same rules apply. Once the feeling of trust is established, it would make sense never to let anything happen to it. When the essence of trust is secure, a new reality forms because you are moved to make decisions from the state of love as opposed to fear.

When you find trust a part of your everyday life, you can literally begin to move to higher levels. When you accept that trust springs forth from your intuition, then growth becomes the art of trusting this intuition.

Passion

Passion is the feeling, the exhilaration, the spice of life. To have passion, to feel love fully, you need to be in touch with your emotions. Now I am not saying that it is bad to be analytical. Whatever you are is absolutely perfect, but what you are really striving for is the balance of mind and emotions.

Babies are passion. They are about the purest of feelings in the here and now. They come with no judgment, for most of them live in a perfect world. When it's not perfect, they don't hesitate to let everyone know. Their world consists mainly of feelings. They have no hesitation in adjusting their feelings when their trust or truth is tested. It is only after many years of hand-me-down ideas that they relinquish their childhood innocence and make decisions on how they are judged by others.

Often you block your feelings because of past hurts. Trust that everything that happened, including the pain, was perfect and exactly what your higher self had planned. Trust that your higher self wanted you to experience the so-called "pain" so that you could work through it and learn trust, forgiveness, and love. Then you would truly understand the meaning of these concepts on a deeper level. You could then release some of your anger and allow yourself to experience your feelings again.

Often you don't express your true feelings because you fear what others think. Maybe you are afraid that you will be judged. Allow yourself to experience all feelings, good and bad, without judgment. If you're depressed, give yourself permission to feel that way because that's part of being human. Release the "I shouldn't feel that way" judgment. If you don't block your feelings, you will feel the depths of the depression. Emotions work their way through you to be *released*. Getting stuck in your emotions with self-pity or "Why me?" creates blocks. If you block an emotion, it stays with you because it can never work its way through to release.

If you experience an emotion, know that whatever you experience is perfect. Trust that this is what your higher self has chosen for you to experience for your growth, and eventually the emotion will work its way through and be released. You will feel clean because the emotion worked its way through without blockages. And when you allow yourself to feel negative emotions, you feel positive emotions with much more vitality. This is how to feel passion, and how you open your heart.

Passion is about doing everything with a real purpose. If you can't put the passion in, if you can't put in the feeling, then don't do it. "I can't have Passion all the time," you may say. Yes, you can! Passion is the essence of seeing the Light in everything.

Parenting

As Beings of Light, you enter into the Earth plane and learn to function within the density of your physical embodiment. Your life journey begins with the interactions you establish with your primary caretakers, most often your parents. The unfolding of this parent-child relationship holds many lessons in your healing journey.

Children born after 1987 are "Shift babies," so called because they actually chose to be on Earth at this time to experience the Shift. Many of them also lived lives during the period when Jesus walked the Earth. They feel that they did not really experience the true focus of a Shift then, so they have waited patiently for this time. Take a good look at these children and see how they differ from previous generations. Do they seem more advanced in using their intuition and somehow act older than children used to act?

In any relationship, especially parenting, live by the trinity of Truth, Trust and Passion. Sometimes you forget these principles when parenting because this may not be the way your parents did it. Today's parents have to do things a little differently.

Communication

In order to talk to children, you have to learn how to communicate with them. Communication should begin when they are still in the womb. I say this because it is the time when the child has two advantages. Firstly, it has all the love of innocence and the comfort of being a little baby, of not knowing fear. Secondly, it hasn't yet developed its "veil." It hasn't veiled its knowledge, and still has all the knowledge of where it came from—the knowledge of its essence. So this little child comes into the Earth plane through the birthing channel and arrives here in the Earth plane with the possibility of bringing forth pure Truth. *The only thing that stands in the way of bringing this energy forth is the lack of understanding from parents whose fears may outweigh their love.*

Now here's where a mistake may occur. A two-month-old baby, lying innocently on its back exploring the many wonders surrounding it, is suddenly brought back to the Third Dimension when some adult sticks a face a couple inches from the baby's face, pokes a finger in its belly, and says, "Goo, goo, gaga." You wonder why the child begins to laugh. It's because you look ridiculous. The child searches its memory for a response and cannot recollect the sounds. Nevertheless, the child laughs and of course the adult laughs, and a pattern of low-key performance is generated.

Another approach would be to make eye contact, and through your third eye (the psychic eye located at the center of your forehead), to send messages such as, "Welcome to Earth. I know it's a little weird over here, and I know you're a bit cranky with us because now you have this body, but welcome here anyway. We want you to stay just as long as you desire, and we'll try to make things as easy as we can for you."

You may ask, "Is this possible? Do you think the little baby can understand English?" Probably a lot clearer than you do. Then again, maybe it is not listening in English either. Maybe it is really listening to your thoughts. Maybe it already knows.

Have you ever heard a couple of dolphins talk back and forth? Do they say things like, "How are you today?" Obviously, they have different ways of communicating. You and this child person also have this same advantage in communicating, and if you use higher skills, the rewards will be phenomenal.

Children communicate on a special level. If you can begin with nonverbal communication, the connection that is established will last a lifetime. For some of you who are just learning about this type of communication, the rewards will move you to new highs. You see, there is no age where this is not possible; children can always communicate nonverbally.

It's a terrible shame, but the flow of verbal energy (when only words are used) can often lead to the onset of fear. Where is it written in your rulebook that in order to get children to behave, they are supposed to be afraid? That's old, passé thinking.

It's the adults who make all the deals, not that they keep them all, but they are the ones who make them. Initially, children believe the deals that you make. Soon enough, however, they learn that most of these deals are not kept. With this new clarity, they begin to formulate how they might follow suit. When you make deals with little people, you have to be very straightforward with them. Their whole life is based on Truth. Thus, only make deals you can keep.

When children are born into the Earth plane, they do not know what lies are, and they don't know what pain is. They don't know how to lie until when? Until they learn it from big people. As soon as big people teach them, they begin to lie and feel the pain that inevitably comes with it.

You might say, "I don't remember teaching my child how to lie." Well, maybe when the child was just a little baby lying in the crib, you said something like, "Okay, if you stop crying, I'll turn you over on your belly." The baby resonates to this and stops. You're so excited by this that you immediately leave the room to celebrate. Therefore, the child begins to understand how deals are made and how they are broken. Some of you will think I'm exaggerating, but the truth is that this is how it really happens.

Where do you think you learned it? You learned it just as you are going to teach it. I know I'm being a bit critical when I talk about lying. "Lie" is a harsh word, right? But the truth is, when you teach your child how to fib, to tell that little piece of "white lie," they get used to doing it. Then what happens? Here's the saddest part: You try to "out lie" (outdo) them. Then it becomes a contest of who can lie the best. When it's all said and done, and because you have more practice than they do, you win. But in truth, everybody loses.

So, start today by telling only the truth. The next time you say anything to your son, daughter, or whomever, ask yourself, "Is it Truth?" It may take years before you never utter another lie to your child, but you can do it. Then guess what will happen when they grow up to be the so-called "big people"? You'll have big people who will no longer tolerate lies.

Can you imagine, my friends, a world where people didn't tell lies? Can you imagine where you'd be? You'd be in the Fourth Dimension.

Start today to make a difference in your lives. Pick the children up, hold them gently, and put your third eye to theirs. Say something like, "I love you," with your heart, your soul, and even your voice if you want to. Just tell them, "I love you." Then, put them back down to rest. I guarantee that you're going to see a wee smile come across those little faces because they not only heard it, they also felt it.

Discipline

If you looked up the word "discipline" in the dictionary, it might read:

> *The overt act used when one can no longer use reason to come to a peaceful resolution when dealing with a personality that uses simple deduction that does not resonate with the acuteness of the adult mind.*

In other words, discipline is the use of force as a logical course of action when you can't get your way exactly the way you want it.

Let's say that you have a little four- or five-year-old running around having a grand time getting into trouble. He's knocking things off tables and tipping over the chairs, and just having a great time chasing his puppy around the living room. Recognize that you probably did that too, when you were that age. But what do you do? He's running by, and you grab hold of his little arm to stop him. Boom! His little eyeballs pop right out through his head and he screams. Although it might not be intentional, you just about pulled his arm out of its socket. Have you ever done that? He starts crying, so you shout, "Stop crying right now or I'll give you something to really cry about!" You made him cry, and then you tell him to stop. Do you see the confusion created in this little drama?

I know that some of you parents out there are going to say, "Yeah, try living with my little four-year-old. Then you'll know that you need to use punishment now and then." In all sincerity, I consider punishment a real foul thing. Let me ask you something. If you have to resort to that, isn't there a breakdown in communication? And with whom does the breakdown in communication start?

"But, Kirael, how do I communicate with one- or two-year-olds?" Do less talking with your mouth and more talking with your heart! All right? Talk more with the heart!

Force should only be used as a last resort, when physical harm is imminent. Look at it this way. You, the adult, weigh in at 130 plus pounds versus the two-year-old at 20 pounds. Is it my imagination or does this sound a bit one-sided? Never resort to physical action as long as the two sides can carry on a dialog. As much as most people do not want to hear it, *force is the admittance that words cannot be found to right the wrong*. Of course, this is not a perfect world, yet you must begin somewhere. If every person reading this would strive to improve communication, how that would begin to change the world!

Relationships

The key to Truth in a relationship is communication. To have an excellent relationship, you need excellent communication. There is no way around this. When you don't understand why the other person did something and it bothers you, talk about it. If you don't understand why the other person did what he or she did, you can get angry or hurt. It doesn't always make sense to you. Each one of you has your own priorities, your own way of doing things, your own values. Some things just don't make sense. Yet to the other person, it may make total sense. If he or she explains to you, in truth, why he or she acted that way, then you can at least understand. It's easy to get angry when you don't understand. If you understand other people's motivation and what makes them the way they are, and you accept them unconditionally, then love flourishes through Truth.

Let's say that two people in a relationship are angry with each other. Their anger has nothing to do with the argument. It's something that happened below the argument. Let's say that the boyfriend is at a party and has an engaging conversation with another woman. The conversation is innocent and has nothing to do with flirting, but the girlfriend becomes jealous and gets angry with the boyfriend. In truth, the anger is simply covering up fear. The girlfriend is afraid that she is not good enough for him, or that she has done something wrong. She is afraid that she may not love him enough to want to make a difference. But she is flatly afraid, my friends. How do you deal with being afraid? Arguing is one way. How many of these games will *you* play in the next 24 hours? The truth is, someone is afraid—not of losing, but of not winning.

Listening is the major part of communication. Good listening is actually an art. It may mean not saying anything but just being there and allowing the other to express. If you often find yourself in the middle, attempting to solve other's problems, then good listening skills will make the difference.

At this point, you may be tempted to go to your significant other and say, "Here, read this section about listening and learn!" Sorry, my friends. This work is not about changing others; it's about changing yourself. Changing someone who does not want to change does not work. Sure, you may express what you learn here with your loved ones, but do it gently, without judgment, and always with love.

How many people tell you that they are in love, but somehow you know in your heart that they are really just trying to accommodate their families or their friends? Let's say Joe and Sally go out on a date. They have a good time, but that's really about all. Then Joe's brother says he thinks the two make a grand couple. Joe's sister tells him she thinks Sally is the one for him, so they go out on a second date. They have a bit more fun—and you see what happens? The trap begins to close. Somebody says, "The two of you ought to get married!" Then Joe says, "Well, I hadn't thought about that, but I guess that's a good idea. My parents like her, and my friends think we make such a fine couple. Yeah, why don't we get married?" A year later, Joe is wondering, "Why did I ever marry this girl? I have such a hard time getting along with her." I would then ask, "Did you really love her?" and Joe might say, "Well, I don't know. I'm not that sure that I know what love is." I would say, "Well then, get unmarried." Then everyone gets upset with me because society says that it doesn't matter if you don't love each other; be married anyway. Wrong again, for there is no truth in that.

I have another suggestion about marriage—that the two of you sit down and tell the truth, the whole truth! You may say, "Okay, I will tell all truths except just this one that I want to keep a secret." Well, then, in truth, you are not finished. But you say, "Kirael, it won't hurt if I don't tell her about the time I was 16 years old and had sex. It won't hurt her not to know that." It will come back to haunt you, my friend, if for no other reason than you know that you did not finish the job. If you have a boyfriend or girlfriend relationship, any lack of truth will become a thorn that will cut you before you are finished.

You live in a physical world, and some of you may believe sex is purely physical. If you think that's all it is, then so it will be. True intimacy is not just physical; intimacy is letting down your barriers. One way to do this is to take one step to the side and release your stuff—your insecurities, your fears—and totally *be* with the other person, completely feeling the other person. Notice that this is just another way of saying, "If you release your fears, love will permeate." Mentally taking a step to the side helps cue your subconscious to actually release your fears.

Imagine being with your significant other and your ego takes a step to the side and leaves behind all your insecurities. You are totally *with* your loved one and just letting your love *flow*. Never force love; just let it flow without inhibition. Imagine just letting it flow through your hug or through the touch of your hand. You'll then know what Passion is all about.

If you have a significant other whom you love for just being himself or herself and not just for what he or she brings to the relationship—that is Passion. When you have Truth, Trust and Passion, you live your lives with emotion—in love. You will then be living within your heart's rule.

And one final thought: This isn't only for marriages, it's for any close relationship. Strive for intimacy in all your close relationships, not just for your significant other.

Metaphysical Business 1

In this chapter, I am sharing that life is completely love. Even at work? Yes, even there. Love can exist anywhere. Wherever you want love to be, you can create it. It may take some effort, a different way of viewing things, but it can be done. I suggest you do it by living by the trinity of Truth, Trust and Passion. Eradicate fear and replace it with love—yes, even in the workplace. "How about the guy who digs a ditch for a living? How can I resonate with love on a job like this?" you may ask. This may sound like a silly question, but are you digging this ditch to get it done, or are you trying to dig the very best ditch you can? Believe me, my friends, there are those out there who want to do their best no matter what the job is.

I don't like to call a business "just a business." I prefer to call it a "metaphysical business." Even if you don't own your own business, I would like you to read this very closely. You don't have to be the owner or the manager to make business more metaphysical. Even as an employee, you can make changes in your own approach to your job.

Imagine that your business is actually an entity, just like a person. Instead of going to your office everyday, imagine you are going to a person. When you enter the office in the morning, if it were a person, what's the first thing you would do? You would say, "Good morning," right? If it were a person you really liked, you would not only say "Good morning," but you would wish them well for the day, or even give them a loving hug. Without saying anything aloud, you can tell the business entity silently, in your heart, that you love it. Do you remember in the section on parenting where I talked about communicating to the baby through thoughts? Well, the business is a living, conscious entity. It can also hear your thoughts. Everything has a consciousness.

Let's suppose, within your living entity called a "business," you have an employee who is not happy with you. Suppose that this employee is actually undermining things. For example, the minute you walk out of the room, this employee says to the person sitting next to him, "Did you see what the cheap scrooge gave us for a bonus?" And the other person, who really is happy with his bonus, says, "Oh, yeah. I guess that was pretty cheap, wasn't it?" Then the unhappy employee says to another person, "I heard you worked extra hours last week. Did you get paid? Oh, you volunteered! Boy, are you stupid or what?" The other person, who willingly stayed late, may say, "I guess I am kind of stupid."

You get the picture: one person running around creating problems. You can refer to that person as cancer, as something that eats at you and eats at you. And if you don't take care of it, it kills you. This little cancer is eating at you, and you don't even know it is there. It's just eating and eating and eating at you, and you're thinking everything is going great. When you walk by that little "cancer," he ducks behind his desk and smiles at you as you go by.

You do not notice it is there. Everything is going along smoothly in your mind, yet your profits plummet.

When you finally realize what's happening, you find this little cancer. What do you do? One, you can pretend it's not there until it kills you. That's probably not the wisest decision. Or you can have it surgically removed. How do you surgically remove a cancer in a business? You say, "You're fired! There, my problem's over." Is it? Is it really? Cancer, like any other disease in the body, affects all the cells around it. The cells around it may not be cancerous, but they are affected. That's why, when the doctors cut out a cancer, it may already have affected other areas they don't even know about.

Let's go back to the cancer in your business. Your employee is gone, and you say, "There, I've cut out the cancer. Everything is fine." What about the person he talked to about the bonus and the other he talked to about working overtime with no pay? They're not healed, my friends. You now have a cancer spreading throughout your company. The company size and how fast the cancer spreads determine how long you will be in business.

So, you may say, "That sounds pretty depressing. What am I going to do?" Well, there is another way—"radiation therapy." You can call this radiation "white light" if you want to. White light is loving energy. Imagine white light given from your heart with love, going to the problem employee. You can transform this cancer and move it to the light where it will no longer be damaging.

From where do you suppose this cancer arose? Do you suppose it's something you did? You are just trying to make your company run, right? So where did this cancer come from?

Let's suppose you didn't pat your employee on the head enough. Maybe when he did a good job, you just expected him to do it, and then you just went on your way. The cancer starts to develop. So how do you eradicate it? You call him into your office and be in your truth. Remember, in any relationship, including business relationships, you should always strive for Truth, Trust and Passion.

The first step is Truth, so you might say, "Look, obviously I could fire you, but I don't want to do that because I believe that the good Creator sent everybody to the Earth plane for an experience. Your experience is to be a part of my company. That being the case, my friend, you are here today. How do we turn it around so you can make the very best of being here? You understand that it isn't about how much more money I can give you because I'm giving you all I can and am just barely staying afloat. I think it's something more than getting more money. I think it's something you need to look at inside of you."

Then, you really start to converse with him. As you do that, you find out where the problems really are. Then you start the radiation treatment. Use white light or love to heal him. It's not about accommodating him; it's about being fair with him and expecting fairness in return. It's about being in Truth. Set the example of honesty. Then expect honesty in return. With Truth, comes Trust.

You may say, "Kirael, I can't do that because I am the boss. I have to raise my voice every now and then. I have to yell at somebody or they don't pay attention to me!" Well, then, get out of where you are because *you're* the cancer. Oops! You can't do that because you own the place! Well, you're not going to own it for long, so you might as well get out now because you are running your company in fear. If you don't learn to change your views about how a company runs, my friend, you're going to struggle.

Now, if you have a very successful company, there's a very good chance that you already know about metaphysics. If you do, then I congratulate you. But what if you want to take it further? Look at your company as though it were a person and break it down into the different body parts. Let's take an average-sized company of 30 or 40 people. Who is the essence, the spiritual, etheric fabric? It would be the board of directors or the owners. The brain is the one who oversees the day-to-day operations, the person who really deals with the people all day long. Who is the heart of your business? If you let anything bad happen to the heart of your business, my friends, well, you can guess what will happen to your company.

Now let's go a step further. Suppose you have accountants. Guess what part of the body they might be. The accountants function like kidneys, right? Because everything has to run through them to be purified and to retain the positive gains. If you have a couple of assistant managers, they are your right and left arms. All you have to do is find out what each part is doing and you find out how to run your company a little more smoothly.

When you have a right arm trying to do the job of your kidneys, it's not going to work, no matter what kind of body you have. Let's say that you are the owner, the spiritual etheric fabric. However, the brain has a cancer cell and is running on half-capacity. You'd better get to that cancer in a hurry. In other words, look at each part of the company as an aspect that has its own explicit job to do.

What if you have just a small two-person company? You can still break the business entity down into body parts. You are the brain. One person can be the right arm, and the other person, the left arm. Does one arm have to know what the other arm is doing? You bet!

If the body is rundown, find out why. With your own body, you know when you're overdoing it, right? You know when you're stressing yourself out, eating the wrong foods, or going in the wrong direction. You know you are going in the wrong direction when things keep going bad on you. You are going to fall down, break a toe, or something like that, right? It's the same with the company, my friends. If your company is not running in the best possible way, then it is going to get ill on you. When it gets ill, you have to heal it quickly.

How many people started out with a wee tiny headache right in front of their head? You may think that if you just leave it alone, it will go away. Then it turns into a giant migraine, and when that goes away, you create a back pain from trying to hold onto your head. Then the back pain turns into a walking problem. Soon, the whole system just shuts down. That's what will happen to your companies, my friends, if you ignore those little tiny headaches. You shouldn't wait for a cancer cell to form.

To summarize, a metaphysical business is a living, breathing, conscious entity. Treat it as a friend. You might want to tell it that you love it every morning and wish it well. You might view the entity as a person and break it down into body parts, labeling each employee as a specific part. This may make it easier for you to determine if each part is operating at its best. If each body part is running smoothly, the metaphysical business body is healthy. If it is not, illness develops.

Metaphysical Business 2

Next, let's look at developing the spiritual aspect of your business entity. If you don't keep a positive attitude about yourself, what happens to you? If you don't embrace your business entity with love; if you don't "white-light" it on a daily basis; if you don't stop and take good care of it, then it surely won't be at its best. For example, if you were working here at the Inward Healing Center, when you arrived in the morning, you would be encouraged to meditate.

Let's suppose you have 30 or 40 people working for you. What if, in the morning, they said something like, "Thank you, Creator, for this place I have to work, and may I do the best that I can today. May I earn all that I have coming to me." If they did that on a daily basis, guess how long it would take your company to shoot right up into the black, instead of down into the red? It would move right up there! You may say, "Kirael, I can't make people do that." No, you can't. You can't make people do anything. However, if you have fear, love cannot permeate. What you would like in your metaphysical business is love. Release your fear and trust that whatever happens is for the highest good.

How open are you with your company? Are you in Truth? Do you keep everything a big secret? Do your employees think everything is going well when actually it is going bad? "But," you may say, "it's the boss' privilege to keep secrets." Well that's the old days. Today, it's about the Shift. It's about doing things differently, because if you don't, you'll just stay where you are. If where you are is where you want to be, you probably don't need to read this. You are reading this because you want to move forward and to evolve.

So that's how to look at your business. That's how to develop a healthy, strong, metaphysical business body and to let the love in the company grow.

Metaphysical Business 3

If you don't like one of your employees, learn to love him or her first. Support him or her in doing the absolute best job possible. Then, if you must, let him or her go. Then it will be all right. If you are the employee and you want to leave your company—first, get so darn professional and become absolutely perfect at your job. When you know you're the best that you can possibly be, that is when you leave. Leave only when you have done everything as well as you possibly can.

Just like in life, if you are working for a company and you want to get out of there in the worst way because you just cannot stand it anymore, I can guarantee that if you looked back, you would find that you had a job just like it before. Guess what? If you looked forward, you would have another job just like it again! You simply haven't learned from the experience. You can look in the mirror, and say, "Have I learned everything possible within the framework of this company?" When the answer is an emphatic, without-a-doubt "Yes! I know it all!" then it is time to tell the boss you're moving.

Let's suppose you're the worker. Your boss says to you, "Okay, today is payday and I've got cash here in my hands. With 100 percent being everything, what percentage did you work for me this week?" Well, everybody is going to giggle at that one. Your reaction is, "You're darn right, I did 100 percent. Give me my money." What if you were struck down dead for lying? If you had to be stand up honest, you might have to say, "Well, I did stretch every one of my breaks this week by about 15 minutes, so maybe I didn't do a full 100 percent. Let's say I did only 98 percent. Oh, yeah, I also came in an hour late. Then I went to have coffee, so maybe I only gave half a day. Let's say I only did 90 percent this time. Then you caught me playing cards. All right, that's down to 75 percent." So your boss says, "Here's your pay, what you told me you earned—75 percent."

It's between you and the Creator if you are telling the truth or not. Will that change how you deal with your company? Of course, it will. If you expected to get 100 percent, how much would you have to put in? 100 percent, right? If you have people working for you, do you think your people might understand that you expect 100 percent from them because you're paying them 100 percent?

It won't take your employees long to do one of two things after that. They will either move on or go back to doing 100 percent. I want you to think about this. Try to get your employees to think about this also. I know this sounds a little funny, but listen anyway. If you had a company of 30 people and every one of the 30 was hitting their 100 percent potential, what are the chances of your company being successful? Pretty darn good. What if you have a company of 30 people and 70 percent of them are hitting 100 percent. What are your chances of being successful? See how quickly it drops? What if you have a company of 30 people and they're all putting in about 45 percent, 50 percent, or 55 percent of their potential? Do you understand why your company is not getting very far?

You may say, "That's great news. Now I know why I'm failing." That's not what it's about, my friends. It's about recognizing that there is no reason to fail. Just like your own life, from this perspective, you understand that you cannot fail. You keep moving in different directions, but you will never fail. Businesses don't need to fail. It's when you give up on them that they don't make it.

How about looking at the entity itself as we looked at the employee of the business entity? What percentage is the entity working at? Is she looking absolutely beautiful all the time? Don't wait until the janitors come along to empty your garbage. If the trash is filling up and falling onto the floor, don't say, "Well that's the janitor's job, not mine. I don't empty trash, I'm a vice-president!" How would you like to be vice-president of the streets, because that is where you're headed! Don't wait for the janitor. Or what about when the phone rings on the desk next to yours? "It's not my phone," you say. "I'm not going to answer the darn thing." And it rings and rings and rings. What if whoever is calling is the one who is giving your company this great big business deal? It could have saved everybody's bacon, but you didn't answer it because it wasn't your phone!

Some of this may sound petty, but it's the truth. When you start to play these games, your whole company goes. Truth. Do you think a good president would empty the garbage? Darn right he would, because he wants his company to grow.

The business is an entity. Treat it with the love and respect you would treat your mate. The minute you lose sight of trying to take care of the people you're doing business with is the minute you go out of alignment. When you're out of alignment, my friends, you decrease your energy or vibration, and then you have to find your way back to alignment.

Bless your business the way you honor yourself and it will get better and better and better. If you honor the business the way you honor yourself, if you love the business as much as you love yourself, you can't lose. It's impossible. You have to win. That's the Creator's way of doing things.

Show your employees that you can collectively grow as a body and you'll get healthier as a body. Show them all these things, my friends, and you will find your entity, your beauty. Your body will work at a much better rate.

Love Mastermind

First, what does "mastermind" mean? A mastermind is when two or more individuals unite with a common thought. For example, there are a couple of very vile, nasty instruments the government is proliferating. One of them is called HAARP (High-energy Active Auroral Research Project). Now I do not want to generate fear, but some of you may become fearful when reading about HAARP.

HAARP is located in Alaska and in Puerto Rico. This instrument shoots an energy beam into the ionosphere that causes molecules to collect together to create a layer in the sky. The beam bounces off the layer and comes back down to Earth. HAARP people tell you they are looking for fossil fuel, but the project has many other purposes that they are not willing to share with you. If you have an interest in these kinds of projects, information is available. Let it be said that the details are not pretty.

I apologize for talking about such things. The whole purpose of this chapter is to replace fear with love. Hopefully, in learning about these instruments, you can replace them with love; you can overcome terror and destruction with love. During the French nuclear bomb testing in the South Pacific, over a hundred people gathered in love at the Inward Healing Center to chant "Om" to stop the nuclear testing. "Wait a minute," you may say. "Suppose something else stopped it." Who cares? It stopped, didn't it? Those who participated know that they played a part. That's all that matters.

Now, a love mastermind is a group of people uniting in love that can change many things in this world. In spring of 1996, 112 people gathered at the Inward Healing Center. Large groups in Massachusetts, Washington State, Florida, Texas, Nevada, Canada, Australia, Japan, and Europe also joined in to chant "Om" together in love. Through that effort, we know that a kink was put into the HAARP program, putting it out of commission for some time. The chanting of "Om" won't stop until someone proves that no harm will come from projects such as the HAARP.

Thoughts actually create reality. Each one of your thoughts is retained in the consciousness of Mother Earth. And for most people, negative, fearful thoughts greatly outweigh positive, loving thoughts. Believe me, not only do negative thoughts affect the thinker, they also collectively affect the world. What if most people sent out predominantly thoughts of Love, Truth, Trust and Passion into the consciousness of Mother Earth? Mother Earth and the universe would certainly be grateful.

At this particular time, as the Earth is raising Her vibration to ascend in the Shift, love becomes even more powerful. It takes only one beautiful thought of love to counteract ten negative, fearful thoughts. Long ago, in the time of Atlantis, when the world was descending from the Fifth Dimension to the Third Dimension, the reverse was true. It took 10 people in love and truth to counteract one negative person. Now, in the ascending Earth, love is more powerful than fear, so take advantage of this. A passionate group of people putting out thoughts of love and truth can effect so much change.

Questions and Answers

I work in a neo-natal intensive care unit with babies who are born several months premature. Are there ways we can work with them in the womb to enhance their life existence?

KIRAEL: Yes, most assuredly. A pregnant woman once came to the medium (Fred Sterling) straight from the doctor's office. The doctor told her that there was a malfunction in the baby. The medium put his cheek next to her abdomen and told her, "This being has to decide whether to stay here or not. You have to be okay with that decision, and then try to encourage her that this is a pretty nice place to be. But if she chooses to go home early (die), that, too, is okay. Say, 'It's okay to go back to God early if you want to. But if you want to stay, I'll be right here waiting for you when you come out.' You just have to communicate with that baby. You have to let the baby know that it can make a choice."

I know that some of you out there disagree with me. But the minute that little egg and that little sperm come together and decide that they are going to split, they form cellular consciousness, and constitute life. So at that tiny stage, start communicating right there. If you are in this neonatal stage and things aren't going right, try first of all to get the mother as clear as you can, because most of the communication is going straight through her thinking process, and passing right into the baby. And listen carefully. The baby can understand you clearly, so immediately start to communicate that way.

Start telling that baby, "Hey, the Earth plane is not as bad as you might think. I'm not sure if you have made your final decision yet. If you're still questioning whether this is the time and space to come to Earth, I can only ask that I be of service. If you're choosing to return home, then as hard as it may be for us on this side, we wish you a safe journey. Please travel in my light. Whatever the choice, know that I'll support the whole of your essence. Whether you are here an hour, a day, or for the rest of this lifetime, I'm not here to judge you." (Make sure it knows that you're not going to judge it right or wrong. And if it wants to go home (die), please don't stand in its way.)

I'm a teacher who works with children with lots of anger. I send them love energy, and I talk to them non-verbally through thought. But they are so filled with self-anger and hurt that it just bounces right off them. Is there anything else I can do to diffuse that anger?

KIRAEL: First, don't be like others and give up on them. That's number one. Then, there is another thing that you can do. Choose a child that you are having a particularly difficult time with, and for the next two or three days, send the white light of love to this child.

Talk to the child the way you would like to have been talked to when you were his or her age. If you ever have a question about how to talk to a child, ask yourself, "How would I have liked to have been talked to at that age?" Whatever comes out, no matter what it is, go with it because the Higher Guidance, my friend, is what will work for you.

Get your higher self in tune with being there with you every day. You should also involve your angel forces. I know that some of my friends are out there saying, "Excuse me? Angels? What are you talking about?" I'm talking about angels being part of the solution. You might try saying something like, "Today, all day long in the school place, I want you to be right there with me because I'm going to call on your Guidance." So when one of these children comes at you and doesn't seem to have a crack in its armor anywhere, call the angels and say, "I really need Guidance quick. I need some words." Then, whatever comes out, let it come. It's called "automatic talking." It's pretty strange stuff sometimes because often you just let the eloquence pour out; it's like being in the third person. You stand back and say, "Wow! That was good!" Yes, it happens, especially when you get the Angelic Realm involved with you because they just want to be of service.

What do I do if I don't have a really strong love for one of my children?

KIRAEL: If you have more than two or three children, almost every family experiences a child born into the family that one of the two parents simply does not resonate with. I don't mean they dislike them; they just don't resonate. You must understand that this child has come in on a completely different set of circumstances and has very little to do with the relationship to the mom and dad. This child comes in to work on a whole different set of experiences. The only way to get into the Earth plane at that time just happened to be to pick that set of particular parents. As time passes, the space between parent and child begins to widen, sometimes to the point where it seems you don't really even know each other. Most times, the parents begin to think that something is wrong with them. Please understand that there is no law that says that just because a child is born unto a parent, the two personalities must resonate.

Even with all this, I'll still offer a cure. The cure is to learn to love each other, not because you have to or because it is in the rulebook somewhere. Go inside the child and really find what makes him or her tick. Don't judge right or wrong, but help purify and perfect the parts of life that allow you to help with the evolution of his or her childhood.

To the child, find out what makes your parents smile and help them smile now and then. You'll be surprised at the outcome. Find out what it is they are afraid of. See if you can't take the fear out of it, not because you owe or must, but simply because you'll find a real win in sharing your journey without the battles.

When you find that glimmer of light and love inside the person, the relationship can begin to build from a completely new arena. This could be the beginning of a beautiful journey.

Is there a good way for me as a mother to better balance the male-female energy to give my son in the absence of a father?

KIRAEL: First of all, let me say that you are doing a splendid job. You have such a good balance within your male-female energy that I don't think your young lad is ever going to suffer from that. If there were one thing I might add, it would be the addition of a "spiritual daddy," or a spiritually oriented male figure.

You see, the child needs to understand the spirituality of male energy, and that's the one thing that the female may have a difficult time teaching. So, make sure that your son is around spiritually oriented men. In that way, he learns whatever he wants to learn from them and he finds a balance.

I have a nine-year-old son who's getting into lying. I wasn't conscious of lying to him. Were we lying to him? What do we do now?

KIRAEL: There is no right or wrong, because you only do the best that you know how. You may, however, begin undoing whatever got done. Sit down and say to him, "Look, I made some terrible goof-ups. One of them is that right along with you, over the lifetime, I've learned how to tell fibs. Let's you and I try to do something really different for the next period of time: a week, 10 days, 21 days, whatever. For the next 21 days, you and I are not going to lie to each other at all. No repercussions, all right? No repercussions! I ask you something and you tell me the truth, but you have to be prepared for my telling you the truth."

You've got to start some place. I know that children will sometimes play games, especially when mom and dad don't live in the same place. Sometimes they will play off each parent, seeking the attention they need from whichever parent they are not getting the attention. So if he stops lying to you, but he is back to lies the minute he is with the other parent, that is his way of letting the other parent know that you all still have a lot of work to do.

This may not be easy, but you have to talk it out together as a family unit. You have to say, "Look, we can't continue on this path. The three of us have to figure out some way to get past this situation. We have a whole lifetime together and we must start someplace. Let it be in Truth."

I have a four-year-old son at home. What's the best way to handle his emotions, such as anger or sadness?

KIRAEL: I suggest that you just bring forth as much of the emotion as you possibly can in a controlled environment, a place with just you and your son. When the emotions start to come, allow them to express themselves in safety. Do you know how many people the medium has to deal with on a daily basis whose parents would not let them share themselves emotionally, especially with men who, as little boys, were told, "Boys don't cry?"

If your son has emotions, bring them out, kicking and screaming. Let them all fly. Eventually, he will figure out that that wasn't exactly what he had in mind. He will learn that he has to start putting words to his emotions. You might not like the words, but that doesn't matter. Hear them. Don't stifle them! Bring them to their fullest and encourage them. Make sure your son is really talking to you. Whatever the emotion, encourage him to put words to it. Listen from your heart to all the words. He will feel your love and respect, and as a result, he will learn to trust this communication process.

I'm a single parent. I have a question about my nine-year-old son. He is fairly hard on himself, harder than I really want him to be. I wonder whether it is something that has happened because of something he has chosen to do, or if it is something I need to help him lighten up about.

KIRAEL: In this particular case, the hardness on himself is a past-life issue. He's having difficulty in this lifetime living up to standards he set in a previous lifetime and can't match. First, tell him frequently how exceptionally good he is just as he is, without having to strive any harder to be any better, that he is absolutely perfect as is.

Second, this nine-year-old is a lot smarter than people—not you—give him credit for. He has an intelligence level of probably a 15-year-old. You can talk to him on a little different level than you have in the past.

Third, help him understand that people progress at their own rate. He's really trying to progress at a very fast rate. Tell him to take his time. He's going to get to the end result anyway. Life is not about how you were born and where you'll die; it is the journey in between. So get this nine-year-old to understand that his whole life, right now, is the journey. Then he needs to accept that his life is just so absolutely perfect, that it's unbelievable! He doesn't have to beat himself up. Daily, my friend, look right into his eyes and tell him that you love him for who he is.

I know that most parents say, "I love you." You may say it in passing, and that's all right, but sit down with him daily, even at age nine. Do it late at night when he's almost asleep. Look right into his eyes and tell him, "You're every bit the perfect son I wanted. I want to thank you for being that way." Then let him sleep on that thought for the next eight hours.

I have a question about punishment. Could you comment on this?

KIRAEL: Good question. I heard one of my teacher friends in the audience say, "Offer a consequence." That's a little stronger than I would like to see. A "consequence" has the connotation of something not being so good. Just remember, life is about gaining experience, and this doesn't always come easily. Sometimes you really have to work a lifetime to get it right.

My suggestion is to sit the child down and have an involved conversation. Tell him or her up front, "This can be a one-way conversation or a two-way conversation. If you respond, it will be a two-way conversation. If you don't, then you just get to hear me talk, so you might as well respond." If you don't get a response, you become a lecturer. Do you know what happens to lecturers? People go to sleep, so you have to get a two-way conversation working.

Teachers, listen. Get a two-way conversation going with your students by asking a question every now and then. Say what you want to say and finish it with a question. Get them to respond. When they say, "Yup," say, "Excuse me, I prefer at least five or six words strung together as opposed to `Yup.' "Then they say, "Excuse me? What did that mean?" Say, "Good! That was good! Now, let's go on." Once you get them in a conversation, you can provide them with directions in exploring choices, learning about responsibility, and feeling good about themselves.

I don't like punishment, and I understand what you're saying about communication. I'm a teacher and I'm having trouble with my students who are nine, ten, and eleven years old. I want them to understand that if they do something wrong, they have to realize that they can't get away with it. My concern is that some of these children are getting into gangs. I've tried talking to them mentally although I don't know if I'm making a difference in helping them understand the consequences of their behavior.

KIRAEL: I'm glad you are talking to them through thought. But sometimes you have to verbalize the whole thought. Tell them, "Look, I don't want you thinking you've gotten away with this. I'm telling you right now, from my heart: I don't want to punish you because that's not what this is all about. However, if you continue doing what you're doing, know that you will not get away with it. You're going to have to pay the price, whatever it is. Hear that right now."

Why are many kids choosing to experience drugs?

KIRAEL: Please don't think I'm being discourteous, but if your child is doing drugs, it's because somewhere along the line, communication has broken down. When it breaks down, they reach out to the next best thing, which they pretend, and is not reality. Drugs represent what is not real. In essence, they're not willing to face their reality. They cannot deal with it, so they must change that reality, and they turn to drugs to do that.

I keep talking about communication. Always communicate in truth. Remember, it is not about instilling fear in them so that they will obey you; it's about honest, open communication. If you are always in truth, trust will develop in your relationship. That is, a passionate relationship with your children based not just on respect but on love, passionate love.

Can you say something about the difference between bosses who get caught up trying to prove something by demonstrating their power as opposed to bosses who just get it done?

KIRAEL: Thank you, that's a beautiful question. If you're a boss who has to demonstrate power, if you have to puff yourself up and remind your employee who you are, then I would say that you already have a major problem. The truth is that in a metaphysical business, you never have to present yourself as the boss. So if you need to put on a little air about yourself, understand that you're going against all Creation. You are not thinking about the good things that you can do with the company but about how to protect yourself in the company. Therefore, you have a serious problem on your hands.

If you would manage your company the way you would like to be treated, you would have a successful company. The truth is, you do not want to be managed by a weakling because that manager has to make decisions. So you want to be managed by a firm manager, one who makes decisions. But then again, you do not want to be managed by someone who is yelling and screaming at you, by someone who is lying to you, or by someone who does not keep his word. So manage the way you would like to be treated: firm, fair, and with respect.

People don't have a job for just a paycheck nowadays. You see, there are more and more people out there who do a job well and need to be recognized. The recognition gives them the energy to say, "I have mastered that lesson. Now let's move on to a new set of lessons." Which means what? It means they elevate their job performance. My good friends, wouldn't it be exciting if you had 20 employees that reached their fullest potential today?

From a business point of view, how does one determine what a fair profit is?

KIRAEL: What a good question! You know it is a good profit when the vast majority of your staff is happy doing what they are doing, when you can pay all the bills and still have a little money left over. I'd say that is a fair profit. If you are in business to amass a lot of money, then I think you are probably going to have a lot of trouble in about four or five years.

A company owner's major responsibility is to supply a space for people to work at a fair income. And if you still have money left over in the bank when it's done, I would say that you made a fair profit.

Could you give your ideas on capital formation and on building enough capital to get a business started, particularly with money markets being what they are now?

KIRAEL: I'd be glad to. The first thing to realize is that every thought creates a reality, if not now, then in the future. Your thoughts are powerful. If you don't have enough money and you think lack, guess what will happen? You will remain without funds. But if you think prosperous and you trust that this will happen, it will happen.

The second concept is that you should never put out the investment capital unless it has a return loop to it. So when you put it out, look at the loop to see how much of it is going to get lost in the loop. Choose the loop well.

Now, my friend, listen to this very carefully: Diversify as quickly, as sanely, and as safely as possible. Although diversification spreads your investment capital thinly, as these loops come back around, one of them may be the big one that you're looking for. You will find that the loops layer themselves in and through each other, so you actually wind up with a fine network of returns.

You know how birds build a nest all intertwined? It is just like a business whose elements intertwine and spiral together. Your investment is then capitalized so that a little twig, fallen off to the side, will not make or break it. It is all interwoven. The interwoven loops make sure they stay together because they are a family and have a consciousness.

When you build a business, remember to foster family-type relationships among the staff members. When you go with family, you know that you're safe. No matter who drops what ball, somebody is going to be over there to help pick it up again. I hope that comes close to your answer, my friend.

When we enter into a business or a relationship, we bring our personal baggage with us. Many times, the tension, conflict, or disagreement becomes apparent when an individual has fears or unresolved issues. How can we begin to address this in a way that is safe for people to understand—so that the heart of the matter is being identified and a sense of support is being demonstrated?

KIRAEL: Everyone within a company comes with his or her own "baggage," as you call it. Learn to recognize when an entity is carrying excess baggage and how to help him or her unload this baggage. Excess baggage is usually full of garbage. All you need to do is clear the garbage out of the baggage. Then you don't need to carry it anymore.

Every company, every entity, should have someone that goes within the company talking to the kidneys, to the heart, to the liver, to the lungs and even to the brain. That person should ask, "How can we discard some of that baggage that you're carrying about?" Talk to your staff. It's not a job, it's a living. If each entity would take time to listen to one another, they would cure the baggage problem themselves. Most people can cure themselves, so when you have a company where everybody can talk to each other heart-to-heart, your baggage will disappear.

If someone wants to give you a lot of money, but the money is ill-gotten, will it affect your business?

KIRAEL: That's a beautiful question, my friend. Who is going to judge the money, first of all? If you know in your heart that it's ill-gotten—let's say stolen—then you will pick up some of the karma that goes along with it. If you have to ask yourself, "I wonder if there's something wrong with this?" then there probably *is*! For instance, if your business entity was a human being, and somebody said, "Here, swallow this cup of poison," would you do it? I don't think so. I don't care if there is a diamond in the cup; if you drink from that cup, you'll die. What good is a diamond if you are dead? You may think, "Can't we just white light it and pretend?" You can, but it will come around, my friend.

Is it really worth even thinking about or getting upset over the HAARP and Boom Box projects? Should we just concentrate on working to improve ourselves and not worry about the things that we have no control over? Or should we be constantly sending white light and good vibrations?

KIRAEL: There, you've got it. I don't want you going out with a picket sign, but I do want you to be conscious of these projects.

You are made up of cells. Each cell in your body has its own thought consciousness. If you activate enough of those cells and you create white light or good thought vibrations, then you can change what is going on in the universe that is antithetical to good. Now, who is to sit in judgment on what is good or bad? Only you can judge for yourself. If you look into this HAARP issue and you don't like it, then send love or white light from yourself into the Earth and into the atmosphere. You will automatically make a difference. For a lot of you reading this, that may seem a bit out of reach, but let me say that all of you will have to start believing that you can make a difference without hurting someone or something. Ask yourself one question: "Is it in the light of human origin?" If the answer is yes, help it grow.

Anger is not going to change anything because anger is the dark side of fear. When you are angry, it means there is something deep down of which you are afraid. Fear is not the answer.

You make a difference in the world plane by working within yourself to eradicate your own fears and then by allowing love to enter. Concentrate on changing yourself and then the world around you will automatically change. When you *become* love, others around you, just by being in your presence, will change. The love will flow out all around you. That is how you make a difference in the world around you—by changing yourself. You don't need to go out and do something major for the world in order to be of service. Just by working on yourself, you are changing the world. And if you want to gather a group together to do something in love, or if you want to meditate together in love, my warmest, deepest thanks to you.

·3·

Reawakening to the Christ Consciousness

UPDATE FROM KIRAEL

KIRAEL: Here is a chapter, my friends, that is going to test your fibers, because you see, in your old belief systems—and I am not knocking them, they are not bad things because that is what you were taught. But in your old belief systems, you've been asked to wait for the return of the Christ Light.

I am to tell you, my friends, the beauty of Christ would never, ever leave you by yourself, because, you see, the beauty of Christ is the projection of the God Creator's Love. It amplifies itself in everything that you do.

And so this Christ we speak of. You could differentiate it, if you wanted to, between the Jesus the man and Jesus the Christ. But I'd rather say it to you this way: Why look past the man to see the Christ? Why look past the politician to see an untruth? Why look past the teachers to see them afraid that they can't or they don't know how to teach? Why not look right into the teacher, and say, "It's all right. We can help you." Why not look into the politician and say, "Why don't you take a chance with We the People?" And make him know that he'll never be alone again.

Why not just open your heart to this beautiful man who walked the Earth so long ago? So much has been said about him. Why look past what's been said? Why not look at what you read and love the parts you love and release the parts you don't? Maybe you don't like reading the part where he went into the hall and he threw the money lenders out. What if that was metaphorical? What if it was that he told the people in that room that day that you shouldn't cross this boundary and make the Lord's house, the Creator's house, a place of money exchange?

What if, my friend, you could have been there the day that he healed all of the people from their grand diseases? What if you could have been there the day he raised one man from his death process? Well, you would have been astounded just like the people that were there. But, you see, like the last chapter, "The Journey from Fear to Love," you wouldn't have been afraid because you would've read me book, and you would know that he was the most magnificent being to be able to carry that most living Light of the Christ Consciousness on your Earth plane. You'd know that he was way more beautiful than he has been given credit for.

But here is the one thing he would have you know—that it makes no difference what path you choose to find the love of the Creator, as long as you walk that path. It doesn't matter who calls you along that path, whether it is religious, spiritual, or anything. It doesn't matter who is calling you along the path because you can't get lost if you have the love to get there. And how could you not have the love when you think of a Creator Force that is the most beautiful expression of Love that could ever be?

So, when we talk of this Master Light called the Jesus Christ, I say to you to read it with your heart. Go back to your Bible again, and don't let those who would try to dissuade you tell you that if you read it in any way but the way it is written, it is no good. You read it the way it is written to you, because if you do, you will find the book that you can really favor. And part way through that book, you may decide, I don't need any more of it, I've got it. And I say it's all right, whatever you choose, whether it is the many paths, as long as you know there is only one that leads you to the Creator. And that's the path of love.

●●●

KIRAEL: Let it be known, my friends, that one of the greatest Masters ever to walk the Earth plane asks for your courage, belief, and willingness to become whole again. Some of you call Him "Jesus Christ." Some of you call Him "The Christ." Some of you just call Him "Jesus." If you don't mind, I'll call Him "Master Jesus."

The Master Jesus energy that was born in Bethlehem unto the virgin Mary and the Joseph entity was brought forth into the Earth plane to make a difference. He was absolutely a beautiful energy. Your recorded history says that He was in His early thirties when He started performing miracles. The truth is, He started much earlier than that, but the miracles weren't recognized because He avoided attracting attention.

At approximately 30 years of age, Master Jesus began His own major shift. Some may argue that the life force energy of Master Jesus had realigned and all that He had begun took on a new and even more meaningful existence. This would be known as the "transition of the life force" and graciously accepted as the Christ Consciousness. For one day, He stood in a line with other human mortals waiting for John to baptize Him in His Father's name. The masses that stood by went into shock as they witnessed His transformation. It seemed that the whole of existence moved into a new reality. Like a thunderous wave, the Creator's Energy swept forth into Master Jesus. Now, the Master became one again with the powers bestowed upon Him, and He went into the world to serve as the healer of all humankind.

It was clear to all who were to record the mission of Master Jesus, that the truth He came to spread throughout the lands was a message of "Healing through Love." These words can be said in less than two seconds. Yet, to this day and time, humanity has fallen short of truly understanding His statement: "Whatsoever I do, so shall you." He really wanted the world to realize that once you remember that love will outlast all the Shifts, then the reality of healing all, including Mother Earth, will become the joyous occasion it was meant to be. No longer will those with power keep the majority veiled by the threat of judgment and contained by self-imposed fear. For it is this Great Shift that will raise the vibration to the knowing that love is the conqueror of all.

A very long time ago, back in the time of the pharaohs, history was passed on orally from one person to another. The books which make up the Bible, for example, were the spoken word for thousands of years, passed on from one generation to the next. Eventually, the stories were written down and translated into many different languages. However, for many reasons, the texts were changed in this process. With the help of the Akashic Record, I want to try to bring some of the information back into alignment. The Akashic Record is a dimension where all that has ever happened, or will happen, is so recorded. Anyone can access these records, but until you are more practiced at it, allow me to translate.

Know that I am not here to offend anyone, especially anyone's religious beliefs. Neither do I need to prove myself right, for I don't need to prove anything. What I will do is try to provide an alternative way of looking at things, for all I'm doing is stating a number of facts that I recognize as Truths.

Religion was only part of Master Jesus' teachings. He truly aligned His energy with the Earth plane so all would become aware that each person is in total mastery of his or her four-body system, which consists of four seemingly separate vibrations: physical, emotional, mental, and spiritual. When you look through the Bible, you will find references to His ability to heal all four bodies. When the alignment of these four bodies took place, miracles would burst forth into the universe.

The Bible relates many stories of Master Jesus and His great work. However, seldom does the interpreter delve into the true understanding of the intense energy that Master Jesus could bring into focus. Those who traveled with Him came together in a vast, undaunted, unified mastermind of thought energy to reinforce the Truth healing of the four-body system.

The question often arises: "If Master Jesus had such powers to heal, why were only a select few and not all of humanity brought into total illumination?" The truth is that there were those who really did not want to be healed. The reasons are many, although most would not admit them. Even in the world today, a disease may be cured in some people and not in others. Always did the Master honor the person's free will. Never was a miracle provided without an impassioned request.

The teachings of Master Jesus are so vast that it would take volumes of the written word to describe His most simple acts. Many stories could be interpreted as Master Jesus sitting in judgment of what is right or wrong. In truth, His was not a ministry based in fear or judgment, so this would not have resonated with His teachings. His real message was Truth, based in Love and Healing. Master Jesus once described Love as the amassing of pure Light thought coming from the Source, cradling the essence of the receiver. How could anyone suspect an energy like this of sitting in judgment of His brothers and sisters?

How many people reading this book find that money or lack of it is a major focus in their reality? How many realize that Master Jesus Himself also experienced lack as part of His reality?

It is said that when Master Jesus was about 14 years old, Joseph, his father, left the Earth plane through an accident. Up until this time, the family had lived quite comfortably as Joseph had provided well for them. Upon the death of Joseph, his employer had promised the family considerable compensation to tide them through the loss. When Master Jesus, accompanied by His mother and brother James, approached the employer, they were told that no such agreement had been struck and therefore no money was at hand. Devastated, they returned to the rest of the family. At this point, it fell upon Master Jesus to become the sole provider. Hence, He experienced lack along with His family, and He found the true meaning of it.

So, my friends, if your state of affairs is not as you wish it to be, simply recall this message and understand that if Master Jesus could find His truth in this situation, then, surely, so can you. Many stories of the Master are available in records that humanity has not yet learned to access. One day these records will be open to all, and many mysteries will then become clear. Truth, as most have always wanted, will become reality.

Learn About the Self

The Third Dimension is an illusion of belief systems. You come here to experience, and all you truly want to do is experience. If you have decided to experience hardship and heartache, then so be it. However, you can change that when you are ready. This is when you will go out into the "magic of a hundred percent;" when you will no longer take shortcuts in your life; and when you will go straight ahead until you receive what you know is justly yours.

Every ounce of energy that you expend here on the Earth plane is to learn more and more about yourself so that you can become enlightened and be one with your Creator Energy again. That is all that Master Jesus did. He came to the Earth plane to experience everything that He possibly could. He learned how to be poor, how to be ill, how to heal, and how to perform miracles. He learned the suffering of death here in the Earth plane, only to reincarnate as proof that life is everlasting and that death is merely transcending to another level of awareness. He was rebirthed into the world plane to finish His commitment to Mother Earth and humanity. The Creator God created a space where the Master would not only be able to experience but also to reinforce His words, "Whatsoever I do, so shall you."

All experiences are allowed, for in the Christ Energy, how could you relate to the sufferings and heartaches that you put yourself through if you were not allowed to experience them? What if the Great Creator God had said to Master Jesus, "We are just going to send you to Earth in full embodiment, and you shall never receive anything but the highest of all. You shall never have any problems. Just go down to cure and heal the people, and do all you want to do on the Earth plane. Then we will swoop you back up into the heavens and back into the Creator's Energy." How then would Master Jesus have had the clarity? Would He have done that by looking into the eyes of people and seeing their pain? Or would it have been better if He had a chance to experience it?

Now, stationed where He is in relation to the God Force, not only has He the knowledge of pain and suffering, but His human essence has actually experienced it. He knows the inner workings of your experiences and how each person must begin to receive the answers needed to move evolution forward.

Judgment and the Review

Judgment seems to be an intrinsic part of the journey here on Earth. Many religious beliefs involve some higher entity standing in judgment of evolving souls. You were probably told as a child that God would punish you or hold you accountable if you did something bad. For the most part, this was just a way to scare you into conforming to the desired behavior. Can you envision the Creator looking on all creation and judging each and every act as good or bad?

In coming to this Earth to experience all that is, making so-called "mistakes" is inevitable. But what if they are not mistakes? What if they are just ways to experience the essence of this journey, and this is the only way it can be done, for the true judging comes on the return to the Source? When a person passes from this reality (death), he or she reviews the incarnation just experienced. This review is done in the presence of the Christ Energy, the higher self, and usually a guardian, such as an angelic being. You review, from a perspective of learning, how you worked through each experience. You go through every aspect of the last incarnation in great detail, and if there is any judging, it will be done by you. You decide whether you could have done differently. If you deem some of the lessons incomplete, you record them so that you can repeat them in the next life.

For example, the review might focus on greed and the accumulation of vast wealth in past incarnations. Your soul's intent may have been to find meaning in a comfortable level of existence by attaining moderate wealth. Instead, however, amassing great wealth became an obsession, and you showed no concern for those who may have gotten in your way. One day, the clarity of amassing wealth will be replaced by the joy of being alive and the ability to do the simple things in life, like being loved for who you are instead of what you have. So, you see, my friends, it is pointless to judge another's wealth.

Path of Return

Along the same lines, someone asked me once, "If God, as we know Deity, is such a true God and such a just and loving God, why would He allow His only begotten Son to come to Earth and live this type of a life, only to wind up being nailed upon a cross and left to die?" I explained that if you look at it that way, if you look at the Creator God and you see Him not to be in the highest wisdom, then you are probably not seeing what is to be seen. It was not a matter of what He did to Master Jesus; it was more a matter of what He allowed Master Jesus to experience. Just like in your own life, my friends, when you call upon Him and say, "How could God do this to me?" God didn't do it to you. You formulated your own programs. You processed your own lifetimes. God is there with His love for you all the way, but you have to reach out to Him. You have to open up your heart and say, "My God, let your son, Master Jesus, enter into my heart." Then, see what happens.

Master Jesus spoke often of the journey of love from the time of birth. All enter the Earth in the purest form of energy, called love, and it is only over time that fear is learned. A child born into the Earth, in its innocence, has no concept of fear until an adult raises its voice in anger. This emotion creates a new and vibrant sensation, which, because of the high energy, is stored in the memory system for future use. Most learn to equate fear with excitement at a very young age, and they carry this into adulthood, never understanding that love has every bit of the same power.

One of the major fears is that feeling of emptiness, the fear that the return to the Creator is lost. At times, it seems the journey is so full of pain and suffering that all will be lost. I assure each evolving soul that this is not possible. Each soul has chosen to return, and only the timing may be varied. The outcome will always be the same, for the Creator welcomes all on the return journey. Remember that all is in alignment with this energy, and in the consciousness that the Master brings forth, no one will be left behind.

Love and Healing

As I have already said, by the time Earth shifts into the Fourth Dimension, humankind will understand the concept of love and will be moving towards the greatest love of all, unconditional love, or *agape*. This is the energy that actually permeates the Fifth Dimension. When you truly understand the meaning of love, you will have discovered the ability to love the Self. This type of love is necessary in order to see any other form of love. It is, therefore, impossible to experience the feeling of love without first loving the Self.

Most recognize that Master Jesus allowed His essence to be focused on this Earth so that His teaching of Love and Healing would become a planetary belief system. Within this great energy that has permeated your Earth plane, everything from walking on your Earth to being the guardian of guardians, we know that those who understand His light and His love also understand that He came here to reawaken our abilities to heal and to love.

Within this awakening, you must understand it is truly, truly about an inner feeling. It is the understanding that love is just a word, but beyond the word is the concept that will bring you into the totality of the beauty you seek. In this, Master Jesus talked about healing the brothers and sisters of the world, and about the healings from all the Great Masters that walked the Earth plane. It has always been the great desire of the Christ Consciousness to awaken each entity on this Earth plane to the understanding that the Christ Energy is already a part of you. It is to understand that the Christ Consciousness is awakened within each, and within that awakening, all that is asked is that you recognize that beauty. It is not to place a great magnificence about it, but just to recognize that it is already a part of you, and that you are part of the universe, for the Christ Consciousness, my friend, is part of the universe.

Changing the planetary thought patterns from being predominantly negative to positive will take a concerted effort. Those who begin spreading the light, however, will find that it is contagious and much more productive than fear. Those moving into love with their fellow travelers find power when Truth, Trust and Passion predominate in their being. It has to do with the essence of your heart energy and your recognition of oneness.

Concentrate totally on enhancing your light. As you do, you light the light within the Self, and it will spread out to all around you.

In the spreading of this light is the understanding of the Truth of Oneness. God can be called many names and looked at in many ways, but there is only one Creator God Energy. And when the Shift is complete and we have returned to the God Energy, we are God.

Light, in its own essence, becomes the reality of Self. In that reality, it chooses the means by which it will vibrate. It will transform itself into many things, all of which collectively return to the Light. In this Light, you will recognize yourself as part of the totality, and, in understanding the totality, you will become one with the Self. Therefore, you are bringing all that is within your own reach into the possibility of lighting the self into the Self.

Many of you who choose to share your learning through trance mediumship or channeling will someday experience what Master Jesus clearly understood. Many who come to teach are put on a pedestal and are loved so deeply that the love turns to fear, which attacks that which is loved, even to the point of death, thereby allowing love to be safely enjoyed again. Simply put, humans will love someone or something so much that they feel they lose control and come to fear the beloved. In fear, they will kill if only to prove its mortality. Then they will honor it, through its memory, by showing love. This is how the Master Jesus was treated. In this treatment, He spoke these words: "Seek not to understand my plight; only search deep in your soul to remember that you and I are one, and in that, my love is yours. Leave by way of entrance, in love."

Questions and Answers

Are God and Jesus like us, except more evolved?

KIRAEL: Well, that's the truth. When you say that they are just like you, it is true. They are Light Beings, in a pattern of light, just like you are. Do not limit yourself to the third-dimensional body that is experiencing this dimension. The truth is, you are a Light Being, or energy pattern, that is part of the Creator or God Energy. Jesus Christ, who came in the form of a man, is the same as you.

Why is Jesus God's Son?

KIRAEL: For the same reason that you are God's son or daughter, my friend. We are all extensions of the Creator Energy. Master Jesus came to the Earth plane to bring new light and to reveal a path of Love and Light. It was your Creator's choice to give you the option to see how you looked. Master Jesus wanted to show you how you could look versus how you chose to look.

Did Jesus have karmic issues to deal with?

KIRAEL: Most assuredly, my friend, He had karmic issues that He created in a lifetime. Understand that this was His first run as a Master. He did not have a lot of lifetimes before He started His work on the Earth plane. He was created in God's image to become a mortal man. By God's image, I mean a being of light taking on the body of a mortal man. He created karma in His lifetime, and He had to work through it just to see what it was like.

Who were Jesus' Guides?

KIRAEL: Two of His Guides were Gabriel and Michael. He actually worked a lot with archangels, but keep in mind that He had access to the Christ Consciousness, which is subordinate, if you will, only to the Creator. He also used the Angelic Realm to communicate His wishes to Mary Magdalene, Peter, Joseph, and all the other Apostles.

Who was a major influence on Jesus during his younger years?

KIRAEL: One of the most influential people on the young Master Jesus' life was a knowledgeable seller of wares who had traveled widely. Master Jesus would listen to his tales of things that were out there. Master Jesus saw that there was more to the world than He could possibly fathom, and He decided that He needed to start expanding His own knowledge.

Little is known about Master Jesus before the age of 30, but it was a lifetime of "trials and tribulations." The Creator allowed Him to process His life like you. However, some of you have repeated the same experiences in your lifetimes, while Master Jesus did not have the luxury of repetition. He had to complete all He could in one lifetime, whereas some of you have been poor in many lifetimes, or in bad relationships for many lives, or ill for the last three or four life-times. Maybe at some point you just need to get past these things and begin to understand that, like Master Jesus, you can heal all.

Were the teachings of the Master Jesus altered after his crucifixion?

KIRAEL: This question raises an issue in history that is usually well glossed over, and answering it will inevitably disrupt a lot of people's beliefs. Therefore, as usual, I urge you to take nothing in life as gospel truth, for everything has room for interpretation.

Peter and Paul were two of the extremely powerful essences that worked alongside the Master. I single them out, for each was to make an important contribution to the Master's work.

Peter was to continue in the perfection that Master Jesus had begun. He was to set forth on a journey that would establish places where those he taught would have a place to continue the teachings of the Christ. The better part of his life would remain faithful to spreading the words of healing, love and a single-minded focus of returning to the Creator.

So far this sounds reasonable, yet when the parts played by Paul begin to unfold, many will come to arms. Why? Because while Peter continued his work, it is widely accepted that the early Christians were being persecuted. At first, this didn't have much impact on the authorities since most of the followers were from the lower social classes. As this began to change, and those with social standing began to understand the teachings of Jesus the Christ, the shift in consciousness resulted in lower revenues to the state. The contributions that had once filled the treasury were being diverted to the churches established by the followers of the Master Jesus.

The Greeks, who for centuries had cultivated the arts and cultures, suddenly found, in addition to having to fight the powerful Roman Empire, that state revenues were somehow dwindling. Neither the Greek nor Roman army was strong enough to fight two battles at the same time: one on the battlefield and the other, which dealt with decreasing revenues from those having found the path of Jesus and all He stood for.

Paul saw an opportunity to slow down the merciless killings of the followers of the Christ Consciousness. He made an agreement between the Greco-Roman Empire and the higher echelons of the new Christianity. The result was an arrangement whereby the government could act as a religious body, and hence, create an illusion of separation between state and church. Over the years, this agreement took on a life of its own, and the balance of power moved to the Church. Moreover, due to the dramatic increase in the number of Christians, the Church actually became the power that guided both governments.

So strong did the Church become that it became necessary to divide the Church in order to reestablish a balance of power. Hence, many of the wars to be fought from that time forward were fought in the name of religion. Is this truth or the ramblings of some seventh-dimensional energy? Your heart will arrive at that answer as soon as it completely ingests the possibilities and begins to place the pieces together. For those that may be upset by these possibilities, remember it is time to awaken to what resonates, if not now, maybe someday soon.

It seems that in formalizing the religion, the Council of Nicea, which established the Bible, left out much of the feminine energy. At what point does the male dominance begin to shift to a more balanced male/female orientation?

KIRAEL: Again, this question opens up much controversy. Even the Bible of today alludes to the fact that it was female energy that was the first to recognize the first reincarnations of the Master Jesus. The Bible also shows that the disciples were reluctant to witness this great event. You may wonder why this great Master would choose the female essence to show Himself to first. Simple. Whether in full essence or as a balanced male/female, the female has always been most guided to clarity through the understanding of intuition. Now, for all my predominantly male friends, please don't take offense.

The female energy of the past has operated mainly behind the scenes, for this offers a much wider vision. Because of this, much of history has been recorded from a male-dominant perspective.

However, the truth, my friends, is that a large part of your under-standing of the past is quite heavily woven in the female energy.

Look at your rulers of today and decide for yourselves if there isn't a female influence somewhere. Can you imagine the powerful leader of a great country having a beautiful, intellectual mate, and not enlisting the vast intuitive essence she might offer in his day-to-day rule? Or a great prince not being influenced by a beautiful princess? So ask yourself whether the essence of those like Mother Mary, Martha, or Mary Magdalene was not in a position to influence greatly the energy of that time.

Lastly, remember that anything that did not resonate in the Master's teaching, such as complete truth, would have been cast aside by this energy, and for that fact alone, this essence must have been kept to the background whereby allowing the focus of the male to prevail.

Yes, my friend, there was, in fact, a female energy that was very influential, but it will take more than my energy to persuade most people to at least give it thought. Hold to the truth that when all is discovered, the female energy was every bit as powerful as any. Let us pray that at least the female side of the great male leaders will always be addressed in the peaceful movement of this journey.

Was the crucifixion of Master Jesus God's plan?

KIRAEL: All plans are that of God. This event called the "crucifixion of Master Jesus" was, of course, more than the ending of the physical life of the Master. It was, in fact, the beginning of the awakening of the masses to the fact that the time you hold on to called "life" is only a small part of your totality, and that a time would come when all life would shift to the higher awareness and become the journey to the new world. History has proven that a few powerful people control the reality of the masses, but trust, my friends, that this will not be the case this time. In truth, the Master's essence will permeate the Earth life, and all will be reminded why the Master was willing to sacrifice His existence in that fashion. Believe that it was not in vain.

Upon his resurrection, when Christ arose and came back in embodiment, was it spirit that took physical form?

KIRAEL: Often the answer to a question will raise more questions. I state without any reservation that the Christ energy has never been apart from human existence. Many seek the Christ Energy from different levels, yet the truth is that this energy is with you at all times.

When the Creator saw fit to offer His Son into the Earth plane, all that was needed was to focus enough energy so as to create a human embodiment. All essence, no matter what form, is the result of this focus that comes in many levels. For instance, when Christ was first witnessed after the resurrection, it was said that He was not in solid form. The reason was, that He chose to bring forth only enough focused energy for those present to identify His essence. Realistically, how could so many believe in a particular appearance unless Master Jesus focused enough of His energy to be seen physically? Again, when dealing with the world of Spirit, please accept that anything can become a reality simply through focus.

There are many reasons why a Master of this great level might choose to reincarnate. Reasons vary, yet in the case of this Master being of such great Light, He never really got to experience the breadth of reality of which a normal human is capable. By using the "aspect" incarnation, He was able to complete the beautiful things He desired but was not able to do as a Master incarnate does. You must understand the theory of "aspects" to appreciate this fully. Remember that each person on the path of enlightenment will at one time or another use this "aspect" reality to bring the current incarnation to a fuller life.

Did Jesus travel to the Americas?

KIRAEL: There is a whole religious group based on the premise that Master Jesus was once in the Americas. He had the ability of "astral travel," and could place Himself wherever He needed to be. Remember that being as highly evolved as the Christ Energy, He could in fact appear anywhere with as much focused energy deemed necessary at the time.

Talk to your American Indian brothers and sisters. When they talk of the Great Light Son, they are referring to the Jesus that traveled astrally. To this day they depend greatly on the spirit world for guidance. The elders teach that any reality of focus can blend into the Third Dimension at will.

After the crucifixion, did the whole world experience the days of darkness or was it just in the area that Master Jesus was in?

KIRAEL: It depends on one's level of awareness as to whether they experienced this time without light. The entire Earth, in fact, was covered in a "light-less" understanding, yet some were unaware of it because it was not time for them to awaken. That is the difference between Shifts. In the one you're referring to, it was a choice as to whether or not one would participate and remember. All will remember this current Shift and, in one form or other, all will be part of the total.

Master Jesus was the greatest healer to come to the Earth plane. How did He do His healing? Was He channeling a special energy?

KIRAEL: Master Jesus tapped into the Creator Energy, and said, "Let me be the conduit for the beautiful light energy that exists within the reality of love." That is how He performed what were referred to as "miracles."

If you will, simply call on Master Jesus. Have Him guide your hands and light your essence during healing. When you call on Master Jesus to light your hands, the Creator to guide your heart, and the Holy Spirit to bring the power, you invoke the reality known as the "Trinity."

Jesus has always been depicted with the etheric fabric, or halo, about Him. The reason for that was His essence on the Earth plane. Although He was embodied through the womb of Mary, at a point in time, He became the Christ Energy and was no longer just Master Jesus of Nazareth. When He vibrated as the Christ Energy, all dimensions were open to Him. His healing abilities were accessed from many dimensions. When He would heal, the halo would get much brighter because He would reach dimensionally to bring the powers in. This is what he brought into the Earth plane; He didn't take it with Him when He left. He brought the awareness of healing with Him in that all might begin to understand the possibilities of following in His path.

It seems that Jesus' healings were instantaneous. How can we achieve that kind of healing?

KIRAEL: When Master Jesus walked the Earth plane, great crowds would come just to be within His touch. The mass consciousness of thousands of people fed into and reinforced the Christ Consciousness. With so much power being emitted from His hands, how could He but heal? A mastermind of creation—the mass consciousness of thousands of people—would culminate in alliance with His reality before His hand. He would place His hands with His own Trinity belief system, coupled with the belief of thousands of people, and the sick were healed instantly. He would lay a hand on a leper, and the leper stood straight. His sores dried and the eyes cleared. All that were present *knew* that it would work.

Master Jesus made the claim that "Whatsoever I do, so can you." In these words there was to be an awakening that this wasn't magic or some sort of individual gift from the Creator. It was simply a message that all are part of Spirit. And the level of clarity you reach is the measure by which you may contribute to the healing of the world. Release your limits, for this dimension will soon be bathed in the essence of this Love.

In breathing of prana and pushing the energy out of the physical body, are you getting in touch with higher dimensions?

KIRAEL: Exactly. Dealing with the third-dimensional body is not the easiest task, and when you bring a certain vibrational pattern to it, things shift. In prana breathing, you actually expand the pattern. We (Guides) actually make you bigger. You may not be able to see it in the physical, but you can feel your body expand because the molecular structure expands. This is how Master Jesus did His healing work. He would tip His head back into the Creator's image to bring that energy down to the very center of His embodiment, creating a tube straight down to the base of the kundalini.

You literally make a tube, a little portal, if you will, that runs right down the center of your body from your crown chakra down to your base chakra, and you ask for it to enter into, and heal, your body. You may still feel like you are solid, but each time, it becomes clearer that you are not. You can then direct this energy out through the hands and the third eye for whatever purpose you wish. You can also do it with your third-dimensional eyes simply by focusing.

I'd like you to speak about those receiving healings.

KIRAEL: Clarity must come to all healers, for until the person seeking the healing enters complete understanding on all levels as to why he or she is experiencing the ailment, there is little chance of a complete recovery.

The truth is that all illness is experienced to allow a certain lesson plan to be played out. A person with an ailment like cancer may have previously experienced multiple lives where he or she was in perfect health. But this may be the lifetime chosen to find out all about this thing called "disease," such as the understanding of pain, of being out of control, or even of the death experience. Whatever the journey, the individual is allowed to learn in whatever way is best suited for him or her.

For instance, if you refuse to accept the diagnosis that you cannot be cured, you may seek out an alternate healer, for what is really needed is a clear, undoubting belief that the ailment will be cured. Then the healer becomes involved when you arrive at this understanding. You now wish to discover how to complete the lessons connected in this journey. At this point, the healer can focus the energy on the cellular memory and begin the rebuilding process. Remember that each cell in the body has a memory of perfection, and when convinced the lesson is complete, each cell can be guided by the light to recall perfection. Thus the healing not only can, but will, begin.

Most people would never block the healing process on a conscious level. This is why it is so important to remember the many ways you can work with a four-body system, recognizing the depths the soul will go to get the experience you have woven into a lifetime.

In order to completely heal, how important is it to know the root cause of the disease in the body so that it doesn't come back?

KIRAEL: The root cause of the illness, the one that started out in the spirit anyway, culminates in the physical. If you do not understand the reality of that, it is very difficult for you to bring the total lesson to a closure. It is in bringing closure that allows the healer to actually do the physical part of the healing.

When we meditate, can we connect to the Christ Consciousness and the Creator? Is this the reason why you encourage and emphasize that we meditate?

KIRAEL: Yes. It's a direct line to the Christ Consciousness. Some use meditation to have an out-of-body experience or to talk to your UFO friends—it's all right to visit them, yet there is so much more that mediation can be used for. It needs to be said again and again that meditation is the *only* way for you to be able to hear the answers to your prayers. It doesn't make sense to ask for things in your life if you're not going to listen for the answer. The only true place to receive the words you seek is in meditation. I don't care if this is repetitious. It cannot be said too many times.

Was Jesus the first embodiment of the Christ Consciousness?

KIRAEL: To answer this, I remind you that all evolving life forms actually exist on different levels simultaneously. The simple answer is no. The complex reality is that the Christ Consciousness existed long before time was measured. So to say that Master Jesus of Nazareth was the first would serve no purpose. Great Masters like this have no set guidelines that they must follow, and this Energy has been used in many forms to move through all dimensions, including your own.

Did the Christ Consciousness take over Master Jesus' body during the last two years of His life on Earth?

KIRAEL: Master Jesus actually started working quite closely with the Christ Consciousness at about 16 or 17 years of age. During this time, they were trying to get Him to do more ministering, so He decided to begin His travels. This is when He started to get more in touch with the Christ Consciousness.

He began to resonate fully with the Christ Consciousness at about the time you are talking about. Mother Mary had told Him from birth what Archangel Gabriel had relayed to her—that He would be special, and that He would lead people to a better life, full of the understanding of Love and Healing.

In its simplest form, was Master Jesus a medium for the Christ Consciousness?

KIRAEL: Well, that's a little simpler than I'd like. One definition of a "medium" is one who creates a space in time to quiet the physical body so that a non-Earthbound entity (spirit) can reduce its vibration to enter and to function at will. The Christ Energy was, of course, a more definitive reception in that, once in place, it would not leave until the journey was completed.

In books about hierarchy, Christhood is mentioned. Is the Christ Consciousness an attainment rather than just an energy?

KIRAEL: This can be answered in a number of ways. Christ Consciousness is the art of understanding your vibration on Earth, in the now. So the answer is yes, it can be attained. The real question is, Would one recognize the awakening? The truth is that this energy permeates all levels of evolution, yet it would be the final evolutionary step prior to understanding the All.

Was Buddha of the Christ Consciousness? Are there other people on the Earth plane who have also reflected that consciousness?

KIRAEL: Buddha was one of the Great Masters to come to the Earth plane. Master Jesus and Buddha were definitely separate and yet the same. They took on different physical bodies and were still, in essence, the Son of God. Actually, there were many of them, my friend, but they are not as well known, I am sorry to say. Not many have recently come to the Earth plane. With the Christ Consciousness, we are actually talking about energy known as the "Son of God." Whether it is in the name of Buddha or whatever you feel comfortable with, the Great Masters are among you.

How will organized religions, which are quite aware of the aspects of Jesus, deal with the Christ Consciousness or the

higher self? Will they understand that they are part of the Christ Consciousness and begin to live that love? My goal is to combine that understanding in an organized religion. I don't want to feel that I have to behave one way in a religious setting and another way with people who are living in the Christ Consciousness.

KIRAEL: Many people are going through this. They want to stay within a formal religion, yet they understand that if we are all part of the God Energy, then we are part of the Christ Consciousness. The only thing I can tell you is this: Keep the search going inside. Keep looking inside. Don't try to convince anybody of the disparity between words and deeds, or of the need to combine them, especially in organized religion. Continue to reach inside and try to find the answer, because when you do, you will no longer have the need to explain it to either side. You will understand them in their own perfection, but most of all, you will understand the perfection of Self. All that the Christ Energy ever wanted to portray in the Earth plane was to find the Christ within, or to find the perfection of the Light of the Great Creator.

In the past, I'm sorry to say, many in formalized religions have used fear to keep you in a certain belief pattern. That fear has broken down over time as people like you have concluded that there has to be more to life than living in fear—whether it be fear of an automobile accident, or fear that you're not a good enough teacher, nurse, doctor, or whatever. This is not the way of the Christ Energy, for you to be in fear.

Formalized religions, by the way, are going to be around for a long, long, time. They will have to go through some changes to allow beautiful people such as yourself to realize that you are just as close to Christ as anyone who wears a black robe. The day will soon come when all are allowed to journey at their own pace, with no pulling or prodding into a belief system. It will be the time when all are allowed to evolve at their own rate. And because everyone will be too busy seeking Truth, they will not judge others as right or wrong.

Different religions are awaiting the coming of their Savior. Will it be the same as the Christ Consciousness coming again for them?

KIRAEL: When you use the word religion, it immediately creates room for debate. If you focus on waiting for the so-called "coming," you are giving up your individual power to discover your own truth. "Saviors," as they are called, never really abandoned the evolution of humankind but allowed each of you to move at your own rate. They have always been here and will never forsake anyone trying to understand the life path more clearly.

You only need to think back to a time when the entire world seemed to be crumbling around people, and in despair, they called out to the magnificent energy of the likes of Christ and were answered in one way or another. You will have no trouble convincing such people that Christ is right here, right now.

I'm trying to bring more of the Christ Consciousness into the classroom. To me, that means bringing in more love energy. I have one child—the more love I give her, the more love she demands of me. Her behavior is worse now. I feel like I've failed her. I'm trying to figure out how to deal with that.

KIRAEL: The first thing to do is not to sit in judgment of her or yourself. If you did all that you could do in offering her this energy, let it be shown to her that love combined with healing is the one way to conquer all.

Remember, not all can handle big doses of love at one time; it's like depriving children of the taste of sugar until they're in their teens. You might think that all you would have to do is to give them a cube of pure sugar and they would think it is the greatest. You might be wrong. They may find that what others seem to love is absolutely undesirable to them, yet if given in small amounts over time, most will learn to want more. How different might this be for the little girl you're working with? Don't give up. The Great Masters haven't given up on you.

Let's take this one step further. If you give this little girl all the Christ Energy, or Love and Healing, that you can, she'll take in whatever she can at the time. As she takes in the Christ Energy, or the love that is sent by another in the Christ Energy's name, it probably will feel good at first. Sometimes it may feel too good and this will create an adjustment period. If you stand by your commitment that you will continue as long as she comes back for more, you will be rewarded with the understanding that love of Self can replace any and all feelings of lack, my friends.

So, my advice for you and your little friend is to show her how to love herself. Then you don't have to keep filling her up. This little girl [Kirael picks up on the child's energy] was physically beaten about once a week, almost every week of her life. Now all of a sudden, her schoolteacher gives her a hug, looks at her with a kind eye, and never raises a hand to her. How does she react to that? That's not common for her and she doesn't remember what it feels like, so she doesn't know if she should accept it or not. So what does she do? She rebels. That scares you off, and she goes back to her beatings. Each time you do the same thing for her, maybe she rebels even a little bit more. But what if, at some point, she realizes that maybe love isn't so bad? What if she decides to rebel in the other direction and says, "I'm not going to get hit anymore?" Just maybe, it is worth your time.

How are angels making their presence known on the Third Dimension?

KIRAEL: Whenever an angel takes precedence in the Third Dimension, you can bet on something happening that will get the attention of the masses. As the Shift begins to gain strength, you'll see more sightings around the world. For instance, you will see more Madonna statues crying and bleeding. These are all what we call "Angel Presence."

The Angel Realm is now working more closely with this reality than ever before. They are using powers to show you of their existence. For such a long time, they have had to relate to the Third Dimension in ways that would ensure that they went unnoticed. The freedom they now share with you is one of allowing their power to become part of your everyday existence.

Their role of actually being able to work within this world has greatly expanded. They now have the ability to embody and work right along side of you. Many angels have chosen to live a fully incarnated existence just to be here to experience the Shift with you. For some, it is the chance to complete a lesson or two they felt they needed.

Whatever the reason they came, be glad they did, because when it really starts to move over here, you'll be in a great space if you are anywhere near them. Don't be surprised if you're living with one as you read this book. The one thing you can be sure of is that there are so many here now that you'll cross the path of one within the next 24 hours. When you do, shine them in the Light, for that is the Truth as they understand it.

To all of you who are just recognizing your essence, I say, "Welcome, and thank you for giving up your home reality to be here to assist in the greatest Shift in evolution ever."

·4·

Photon Energy

UPDATE FROM KIRAEL

KIRAEL: Photon energy. This is an exciting, an impassioned chapter. It is right on the edge of exciting when you look at it with passion, and I will tell you why. This is the chapter that explains how some of the things that you have lived with, oh, my gracious, just aren't the most proper. You've got to know that. But it also tells you all the way through, that you, or what we call We the People, can make the changes.

Photon energy, my friends, is something that once you gather it, once you understand it, you know that they can't force into a pipe; you know that they can't make it follow a wire. It's just there, and it will do everything that your fossil fuels do now. Oh, yes, you can use it as communication forces. Do you realize that?

If I had the time and the wherewithal in this book, I would teach you right now how to put one little particle out on your forehead, right on what you call your third eye. Then I'd ask you to push one little particle out behind it, and then another and another until you had just a wee bit of a laser beam coming out of your third eye. And then I'd ask you to connect that into the photon energy and watch it pick up and go exactly where you want it to go. Make it turn loop-de-loops if you wanted to. Make it fly up into the sky and down into the base of a tree. Or send it around the world and talk to your friends over on the other side of the world. Because all you've got to do is think it, and it will follow through that photon energy like, what you'd call today, a bullet train. It cannot be stopped.

And then I'd tell you this about your photon energy—that one day, you'll be able to take a handful of it and mold it into a beautiful ball. You'll be able to feel it. You won't be able to see it, me friends; you don't need to see it. But if you molded it into a ball and you held it up to your lips, and you kissed it with love. And you sent it up and it floated up in the air in front of your face, and you said to it, "Go find the one I love the most," it would just disappear. And wherever that one is that you love the most, it would appear right before it and touch its lips and be gone. This is photon energy. This is the Great Shift.

So in this photon energy, you'll get all caught up in the photon belts and how all of it is going to unfold. And then you'll do one thing that I wish you wouldn't: you'll want to stop right where you are and wait for the photon energy. Don't you know, my friend, you can't do that.

You've got to finish up this journey. You've got to get all of these lessons out of the way. But shouldn't this act as some sort of an incentive? I believe it should. That is why I wrote this book— as an incentive, not a fear.

Let me add a little more here about photon energy. If it becomes clear to the consciousness of the human world that you have something available to you that will power your computers, power your vehicles, whatever vehicles you choose to have. If you have something available to you that will move you through space and time, then how are they going to hold you up for a raise in prices when it is all yours for free?

Lastly, even more than that, just imagine with me as you read this: If you didn't have oil products to fight about, maybe you'd stop fighting about everything.

•••

KIRAEL: Long before time was measured and recorded, in what you would call "deep space," an energy source known as "Photon Energy" began its trek to meet with the planet Earth. The outside edge of the Photon Energy is called the "Belt," and it is currently just beyond your Earth's atmosphere at this point. This belt is not really moving to Earth, but Earth will at a prescribed time pass into and through this energy. In this chapter, I describe the approach of the Photon Energy, its mass, its uses after the Shift, and its effect on human beings and Mother Earth. Journey with me now as I introduce you to this magnificent process and reveal it as a path of beauty rather than of fear.

Although the Photon Energy has been observed by the Galactic Brotherhood and overseen by the Angelic Realm for many thousands of years, the actual size and nature of this energy field cannot be readily measured in human terms. Consequently, higher powers will align the energy into something that is compatible with Earth energy. This energy alignment has been used in major Shifts to actually bring energy to a system that can no longer operate on its current energy. The new energy has powers to extend life, because its molecular structure realigns the human body into what is known as a "light body." The Photon Energy will allow human beings to work on their new mission and to attain the growth that has long been forgotten.

The arrival date of the Photon Energy has changed at least four times. You must be wondering how anything this significant could have such a variable schedule. The reason for this is simple. The arrival of the Photon Energy is directly influenced by the rate of spiritual awakening of Earth's population. Although this event is planned for soon after the turn of the century, the actual date depends on individuals like those who came together to assist in the writing of this book to help in the awakening of the people.

The awakening of the masses to the plight of Mother Earth can and will influence this time process. An overwhelming abundance of Earth's foliage has been removed, great quantities of refuse have been poured into Her waterways, and millions of tons of foreign substances spewed into Her atmosphere. As Mother Earth's rotation and pulse (heartbeat) are healed, She has reason to slow the journey so that we may align more of the population to ready themselves for the most exciting event in recorded history.

Photon Energy Is Light

Let us introduce the upcoming phenomenon called the "Three Days of Darkness." Doesn't that term conjure up some fear? Well, my friends, it should, because this is where the real action begins. Although we speak of darkness, be clear that Photon Energy is, in fact, light. That's right, actual light, the essence of light beings.

The darkness will occur as a result of Earth's entry into the Photon Energy. The outer edges of the Photon Energy Belt are extremely dense and define the shape of this unique energy pattern. Therefore, it will take Earth about three days to pass through the Photon Belt before She emerges into the light of the Photon Energy.

When I speak of "darkness," this is not normal nighttime darkness. This darkness is unlike anything ever experienced by humanity. It is so dense that it can be felt. You could hold up your hand within inches of your eyes and not be able to see it. Along with this darkness comes an unimaginable cold and empty presence that will permeate the Earth. The reason for all this is that as Earth enters the Photon Belt, it is almost completely cut off from the sun's energy.

Once through the Belt, the darkness will be followed by brilliant light. The Photon Energy light will illuminate Earth for 24 hours a day, although time will be measured differently than it is now. Upon entering into the new light, most will struggle, because everything will have changed, including the appearance of Earth after having gone through the beginning stages of cleansing. Those who have prepared themselves for this event by learning simple concepts such as centering through meditation and heightened mental clarity will become the light for others to follow. In those first few days, all will seek to understand what has happened. Initially, it may be somewhat difficult to understand because Earth will seem so perfect. Believe it or not, just the reading of this work and understanding its concepts will allow you to establish a new way of life to reshape Earth.

The Backdoor Syndrome

Let me bring to light what I call the "backdoor syndrome." Whenever pressures begin to mount, many choose to run out the back door. If they have a choice to complete the experience or avoid it, many will cut and run. The reason is simple: Fear of change and growth; and the safety of sticking with the known prevent some from seizing the opportunity.

If this topic irritates you, really look into why. Safety is quite possibly the main reason most people repeat painful experiences over and over in a particular lifetime. How many people do you know who, when a relationship turns bad, leave, only to begin another one just like it? The situation is the same, only the faces change. Why would anyone want to go through this repeatedly? As with all other lessons, when the truth is understood, the repetitions seem silly.

Look at your own life and see if you are prone to dealing this way with your major life issues. You definitely won't be in the minority, for in truth, most spend lifetimes trying to get even the smaller lessons learned, while others seem to almost devour multiple learning in one lifetime. Either way, please remember that it is the *journey*, which is all that really needs to be experienced.

The information in this particular chapter may generate fear. Some may use it as a reason to avoid their current experience. I assure each that this would absolutely be the most devastating thing you could do. I use words like "absolute" and "devastating" for emphasis. The truths shared here could mean the difference between success and even greater success. This new energy brings the potential for evolution. You would want to continue with those experiences that have the ability to secure a higher level of truth in the early stages of growth in the Fourth Dimension.

Clearly, it remains important to learn all that is possible on this side so that you awaken in this new energy with the highest probability of fulfillment. It is really not a question of whether you will, for there is little doubt anyone would choose to miss this experience. The only question is how much of the current plan will you bring to this new alignment. This sets the stage for planning the vast new awakenings possible in pure Truth. Experiences lived over and over in the Third Dimension must be brought to completion before the actual ascension of Mother Earth.

Humans are, by true nature, evolving entities on a vast journey of experiencing any and all possibilities. That, my friends, is an emphatic "all possibilities." Each has assured the Self that no lesson will be only partially learned, for incomplete understanding would not be of service to a soul wanting total clarity. Therefore, in order for all possibilities to be experienced, the search for complete understanding must involve many different levels at the same time. Attempts to shortcut by not completing the experience totally will result in taking excess baggage into the new reality. With all the beauty to be experienced in this new energy, you surely don't want to be laden with old experiences. Learn with a new zest and eliminate wasted time in the Fourth Dimension.

Prepare for Manifestation Now

Photon Energy is of a much higher frequency than most are accustomed to, enabling things such as instant manifestation of thought here on the Third Dimension. As the human essence moves towards the actual Shift, many will experience what appear as waves, or brief encounters, with this Photon Energy. This may stimulate increased awareness, exhilaration, and clarity, followed by a feeling of being let down as the energy phases out of Earth's reality. Therefore, it is essential to maintain clarity and purity of thought through meditation and being in the now.

The reason I am addressing preparation is to make sure you understand the phrase "in the now." People often live in the past because they somehow feel safe, or they pretend to live in a false security known as the yet-to-be-manifested future. The way to manifest the future is to focus in the now. For example, when you wish for something in your life, you usually see it in the future. This is generally a mistake because the so-called future never quite becomes a reality until it actually becomes "the now." In this case, wouldn't it make more sense to create all desires in the now?

A final note: What if you align your energy based on the fact that the Shift will take place at some specific time, and it does not occur? What if it goes into next year or the next? What will happen to all that you were supposed to have completed? You will have had ample time to complete experiences that were established by your higher consciousness so that they do not have to be carried forward. This leaves the evolving soul only the universal truth of rising to a new and exciting level of awareness. Live your life in the now. Continue to experience the current journey, exploring all that is possible.

Timelines are of little importance when you realize that life is about completing your current experiences. When the Photon Energy actually merges with planet Earth, those who have completed their experiences will be so ready that the only thing left is the thrill of the experience.

Remain Centered

Following this simple advice will minimize confusion and dispel fear. Remain centered, and the body will raise or lower its vibration to compensate for all that's going on around you, because, like some of our animal friends, humans have built-in defense mechanisms that assure the perfect vibration to survive changes.

Over time, humans have become lax in the desire for new levels of understanding—except in the matter of amassing large quantities of money. If you are not meditating, this might be a good time to start, for an understanding of the four-body system is gained from this practice.

Meditation clarifies conscious thought processes, allowing you to contact your higher self at will. It also allows you to contact outer realities that you would not otherwise recognize because the linear nature of thought in the Third Dimension prevents you from seeing past the veils. Meditation, coupled with prayer, allows you to begin to remove the veils and clearly receive the insights to align with your experience. The increased clarity of your experiences is proof of what you may achieve through meditation and prayer. Without connecting to your higher self, you will continue looking through the veil while denying your larger Truth, Trust and Passion. Meditate, my friends, meditate.

Time and Compression

In the Fourth Dimension, the Photon Energy will create many new and exciting journeys, one of which is the measurement of time. Most of you sense that time is seemingly speeding up, even in this reality. You haven't seen anything yet. Under the influence of the Photon Energy, time will be completely reshaped. For instance, the average life span of humans may be extended to over 100 years, while the rate of breathing will fall to about three to four breaths a minute. How's that for drastic?

When the Shift happens, realize that all third-dimensional experiences such as relationships, money, and governments will virtually shut down or will be subject to massive change on many levels.

Already, nearly everything you recognize is moving at an increased rate of vibration, and you are having difficulty understanding where life is disappearing to. Well, congratulations. Now you know: it is all part of the Photon Energy. Love each day that you are here. Love the now. When you come from love, you do not look forward to the next day, but look only at the reality of now. If you want to dream about tomorrow, have dreams and enjoy them, but live in the now. If you do not like speeding the way you are, then slow yourself down. Take on one experience, play with it, dissect it. Then complete it so you can move on to the next. Everything is a choice.

Alternative Energy Sources

The Photon Energy that you will be entering into is an unclassified energy source. It offers independence from fossil fuel and other energy sources that have become essential to maintain your current way of life. This is one of the ways the so-called "powers-that-be" have curtailed your growth. However, you will not need these sources because Photon Energy will meet your power needs.

Anyone can harness Photon Energy to provide a powerful source of energy that will permeate your entire planetary system.

Photon Energy, right now, is something that is being explored by only a few brave scientists, but they have not yet even begun to scratch the minutest possibilities.

There will be no monetary charge for using Photon Energy since it will be in total abundance. There is no way anybody can take it captive and keep it. Therefore, no one person or group can use it to control or to charge some astronomical figure and, again, hold the population hostage. Those that try to control it are in for a major surprise.

During the conversion period from fossil fuels, you may feel lost trying to figure out how to use this energy. Again, don't panic! To moviemakers: Stop depicting the Galactic Brotherhood as monsters because they will be the answer to your harnessing and directing this new energy. We talk extensively about them in Chapter 6, so for now, just accept that they will be of service.

Atmosphere

The Photon Energy is already intercepting your Milky Way Galaxy and blending with it. Be very clear: the Photon Energy is no longer *out there*. The outer edge of the Belt has already reached Earth's atmosphere and is affecting not only your planetary system but also many planetary systems around you.

The star system, Sirius, is already greatly affected by the Photon Energy Belt. This is good because the Sirians on Earth will teach you what they know about Photon Energy. Previously, Sirians were known to be very aggressive, but the beauty of the Photon Energy is diminishing their aggression.

The Photon Energy will have a positive effect on the Earth's atmosphere. The very air you breathe will be photon-injected, and breathing will become much more important because you will actually be able to funnel the Photon Energy through the crown chakra (the top of the head) into your body for cleansing. The Photon Energy will be one of your main food and vitamin sources, much as your health foods and vitamins are today.

Certain new functions are currently unknown to you. For example, you will adjust your light-bodied energy patterns with the influence of this new energy. You will adjust frequencies of your vibration and become less physically dense. In addition, unlike today, meditation will become a way of life.

There will be periods of time where you will simply ingest the Photon Energy by changing the vibration of the body structure and distributing this new energy throughout your entire body. You will revitalize each organ on a scheduled basis in order to avoid disease, and you will focus on new and challenging experiences, such as new forms of travel that are dependent on the quality of the atmosphere.

Water

The Photon Energy will have a marked effect on your oceans and your waterways because the energy will be absorbed into the waters. Many of the impurities in the waters will not be able to co-exist with Photon Energy and will be absorbed by it. This is part of Mother Earth's cleansing. However, it will proceed more slowly than the rest of the changes that will take place, because over the last few hundred years, the waters have become polluted to the very core, and healing the oceans and waterways cannot happen overnight. As miraculous as this energy is, some cleansing will require the help of the population.

The Photon Energy will appear to expand water, so it will seem that you will be using more. However, in fact, you will be drinking less than you currently do because your real ingestion of water will be energetic. During the switchover period, the Photon Energy will allow you to absorb, through breathing, the moisture needed by the body.

Like everything else, there will be a period of adjustment. However, the outcome will astound even the most progressive thinkers of today.

Human Body and Consciousness

Changes in the human body will take place over the first 15 years after the Shift. Years will pass much more rapidly than at present even though they are already moving quite rapidly. Because of the light body make up, you will be less concerned about your waistline, for that will not be part of the experience. You will look at beauty in its entirety in a completely different way.

Eventually, you will look similar to how you have envisioned your galactic brothers and sisters (although your visions are based on a somewhat distorted reality). As for the actual appearance of the human body, there are those who may be disappointed at first, but overall, you will come to love the new look.

As for spending time and money on hair preparation, forget it. You will be able to choose your appearance as the need arises because that's just how you will vibrate. Aging will be slower than you might imagine. Impatient? Sorry. It is a process for which you will just have to wait.

Brain Capacity

Because of the increased brain size, the cranium will have to expand. The Creator was planning ahead when the bone structure at the top of the head was made to look like a zipper!

Most humans use only about 10 percent of their brain in the awake state, leaving a lot of remaining brain capacity. As people align with the nonphysical realities, unused capacity will be increasingly used.

After the Shift, even those working with lower vibrational experiences will use 60-65 percent of their brain capacity, but it will be only a matter of time before they, too, increase the percentage of use. The difference is only a matter of individual evolutionary choice.

Animal Life Forms

Because it is such an evolving energy, the Photon Energy is not supportive of non-evolving species; therefore, many species will not survive. Anything that is no longer able to evolve will be removed from service here on the Earth plane, for those that have reached the end of their evolution have no further reason to exist. They will be unable to tolerate the Photon Energy because of their remaining density.

All of you dog and cat lovers can breathe easy because dogs and cats are still learning and evolving, and will therefore be going through the Shift with you.

Plants

Plant life is committed to be here to be ingested, to sanctify and refurbish your physical bodies. Plant life is the ingestion ideal and the atmospheric ideal to which your Earth plane must evolve. Plants that have been so diligent in trying to survive on sunshine and oxygen-type atmospheres will be enhanced immediately once the Photon Energy arrives because its energy enhances the lightness of the Earth's atmosphere. So plant life will ingest this energy within hours of its arrival.

Plant growth will increase by up to 20 percent in the Photon Energy. More importantly, the nutritional value of plants will increase. Your eating habits will change rather drastically as most of you will ingest plants to sustain human life. Vegetarians will be much happier, and meat-eaters will struggle for a short time. Remember that most of your energy will come from Photon Energy ingested through prana breathing, with the need for food greatly diminished.

The Photon Energy can only be used for the highest good, so long-term effects on the Earth plane are absolutely beautiful. Photon Energy is unlike anything you have ever seen, heard of, or ever been a part of, and it should be fair warning that energies like me have come to this dimension just to tell you of it. We journey here with the Truth, and try to get you to Trust. As the Passion is created, all will find the path to unity.

Questions and Answers

How is Photon Energy going to impact the crystals of Mother Earth?

KIRAEL: Humans are fascinated with crystals because each seems to have its own personality, special feeling, and a way of working its way into your heart. Because the Photon Energy is light itself, it will bring a new and brilliant luster to each species of crystal.

Crystal vibration will be enhanced so that even if you do not often interact with them, you will be drawn to the life within this living essence of the Creator.

What effect will Photon Energy have on a fetus in the mother's womb?

KIRAEL: The effect will be quite profound. Since the unborn child will evolve at an accelerated rate, the Photon Energy will create a lighter space for the purpose of carrying the child to term. The average time in the womb will drop to about six months of Earth time. Before entering the womb, the entity will have the chance to communicate its life plan to the parents. This will reduce the current breakdown in communications, such as wrong child-to-parent situations. The Photon Energy will also enhance transfer of DNA encodements, thereby allowing a perfect plan to be worked out even before the birth takes place.

While in the womb, the practice of inner stellar travel will be the rule as opposed to the exception. Through the light energy, the parent and new child will be brought together in this mode of travel, so when the actual birth takes place, the union will be much more complete. For a change, it will not just be with the mother, since the father will also be able to travel, giving the male energy a chance for a more complete bonding. Until this energy arrives, it should be made clear that parents, especially the father, should try to join with the baby's essence through meditation and sleepstate programming. Most will be pleasantly surprised with the outcome of this process and will want to continue to the highest possible reality. Have a wondrous journey.

Will the Photon Energy affect human behavior?

KIRAEL: The Photon Energy will not only affect human behavior but will change the very essence of how you use the current body system. For starters, because of this lighter energy, you can change your appearance. Currently, the only things that hold you from doing this are physical density and beliefs. Once fully involved with this new energy, a new knowingness takes over, and you become confident in your new abilities. Within the practice of meditation, you will breathe through the dense vibrations and begin to experience this new energy by learning from the teachings of the Angelic Realm, who are in position to become your teachers.

How long will we remain in the Photon Energy?

KIRAEL: The answer to this may come as a shock to some. The estimated time is 2,000 years. Does that have a familiar ring? So, do not worry about it because none of you will be embodied when the planetary system leaves the Photon Belt. While each of you is a pioneer of the present, you will leave much for future generations to explore.

How do angels and light beings use the Photon Energy in their mission in this universe?

KIRAEL: What a beautiful question, for the Angelic Presence is wanting this answered. Angels already permeate all realities although most are not seen but only felt. With this new energy, they will be able to focus their essence so that Earth beings may interact with them. For the most part, they will continue to be seen as patterns of light yet able to appear at will. Because of this light-injected space, they will be much more inclined to appear in their natural flying state. Believe that they are ready to move the experience ahead because interaction is the ultimate quest.

As for the light beings, there is little to be said, as this new energy is made of a Light source. So, in a sense, the interaction is with you yourself. Light is the essence of all life forms.

How best can the third-dimensional carbon-based body prepare to integrate the Photon Energy into its evolutionary process?

KIRAEL: The answer is simple: Meditation! Every time the chance to speak of meditation comes up, please do so. Some may think I am being repetitive, but be assured that meditation is the closest you can come to enjoying the new energy. In a good meditative state, you can begin to feel and learn how to interact with this energy to be prepared to move ahead. Remember also that while you are in meditation, this new energy is most discernible.

As the Photon Energy surrounds the Earth plane, how will

this affect the more highly evolved species of dolphins and whales?

KIRAEL: This new energy will bring humans up to a level where they will begin to understand the communication of these loving creatures. It will also allow the dolphins and whales to release the vast knowledge they have carried for millennia. The whale, with its huge brain capacity, has been carrying historical facts from one generation to the next with the understanding that eventually humanity will no longer look upon these gentle giants as prey and begin to relate to the treasures they hold. This energy brings with it truth and understanding of love, and once the treasure of this animal is unveiled, the masses will honor them for the value they bring.

As for our dolphin friends, they will be the teachers of this dynamic power of sonar they currently use. This alone should create a new and perfected way of journeying, while allowing all to feel the power of self-direction. In their present state, they can already understand most human speech, although it is not in their best interest to let it be known at this time. They actually have so much to offer that it would fill a whole work of its own. For now, just understand that dolphins occupy a very magical space in the Photon Energy, which will be revealed at the right time. Love them and protect them as they are, and one day the rewards will honor human existence.

Would you comment on the Photon Energy and how it relates to the Christ Energy?

KIRAEL: To demonstrate how the energy patterns of these two are similar, it must be understood that Master Jesus was at all times surrounded by a vibrational essence unnamed by humans at the time. This powerful vibration was unlike any other in that it had the ability to penetrate even the densest patterns of mass by simply becoming one with them.

If you would understand that when you take certain energies, like that generated by love (the strongest force known to humans in the now), they have the ability to affect only that which will accept them. For instance, if you are sending love to one who is not receptive, be clear that this energy will not resonate with the vibrational essence of this person. The love energy will be deflected and continue on its path until it finds a receptive mass that will allow it to blend. The energy that Master Jesus brought forth could penetrate anything. Those who were experiencing the lower vibrations of anger, hate, and fear were unwilling to receive His love, and found His presence quite uncomfortable. This often resulted in unpleasant experiences for the Master, for when one who is operating in the lower vibrations is suddenly confronted with the most powerful energy known to human, there has to be a reaction.

The Photon Energy has a comparable high vibration in that it does not need a receiving mass to permeate whatever comes into its path. Know that as this book is being completed, this new energy is already starting to wave over the Earth. Those in the process of ascension and vibrating at higher levels will quickly adapt to the Photon Energy. They will understand that this is the energy of the new millennium. Those who continue to hold onto the lower vibrations will feel the need to resist the Photon Energy, hence amplifying the conflict and escalating the disruptive experiences.

Simply put, this new vibration is being brought forth for those who are resonating with change. This change is the understanding that new and exciting possibilities exist. It is in the knowing that now is the time to ascend to a new level where Love is the answer. The questions filling the Earth plane as we begin the greatest journey known to humans are, in fact, the awakening to the Shift.

·5·

Evolution of the Soul

UPDATE FROM KIRAEL

KIRAEL: The "Evolution of the Soul" chapter is one that I love so much because it gave me the grand opportunity to allow you to feel as though you could never be "less than" again. It allowed you to discover that the love inside of you is the same love that the Creator has that brought you to be on this planet.

What I didn't tell you in this chapter was this: I didn't really make it clear that when the Creator calls upon you and says, "I got a journey to the third dimension," oh, my God, you celebrate. You cannot believe the celebration—you, your whole soul family, everybody around you. (You'll read about soul families in this chapter.) You get to understand that you are going to go and serve your Creator. Oh, it gets no better.

The first thing that most of you did after that was call me. For most of you reading this book, the first thing you did was say, "Master Kirael, I am going to the Earth plane, and the Creator said you are going to be there with us." And I said, "Yes, but don't forget—that you will forget for some time. You won't remember all of the beautiful things that you are going there to do."

The journey of the soul, the evolution of the soul, my friend, is the particle values of your Creator incarnate. And that's you. You are those particles. And don't you know, as time unfolds, you are going to start to remember it one day. You are going to pick up this book and it is going to have "Kirael" on the front cover, and you are going to look at it and say, "What is that?" And you are going to set the book down and something says, "No, you can't; you've got to pick it up." And here you are reading it now.

Oh, it'll find its way to you, my friends. It'll find its way to you. If a friend has to stick it under your nose, that's what they'll do, because, you see, the evolution of the soul is to show you that the Shift can't fail. It cannot be about whether you might or might not make it. It's about whether you choose to be part of it.

And hear this: Because it is the evolution of the soul, it is when you feel the pain the most. You just had, oh, maybe a terrible argument with your best friend. Or maybe you have looked in your pocketbook and there is no more money inside of it. That's when the soul begins to evolve. It begins to say, "No more. I'll not be involved in a bad relationship because I have a soul, and my soul is connected to love. And in love, I deserve so much more. I'll not be broke again. I'll not be poor. I'll do the things on this Earth plane that I want to do, because I'll do the journey."

In the evolution of the soul, you will come to know that no matter how much you can think, that is exactly how much you can have. Don't ever lose sight of it. When you read this chapter, you are going to hear about all of the different levels of consciousness and such, but remember this: The next time someone says to you, "There is no answer to this," you look them right in the eye, and you tell them, "Wait a minute. I read *Kirael: The Great Shift*. And that book says that if it can be a problem, it must have a solution. And if it can be angry, it must have been happy at some point. And all we have got to do is put one foot down in front of the other. We have to believe that we can evolve our soul."

And then one day, when you've done all of the evolving that you want to do, you will merge with me or one of the other great masters, and we will all go sit with the beautiful Light of the Creator. We'll bathe in sound that you have never heard. We'll feel the lights and the colors as you've never seen. We'll find that it was all worth the journey. And we will be called upon by the Creator to stand up and be counted as the particles that said "Yes."

•••

KIRAEL: Everything that exists is made up of energy in one form or another. The spark of life (soul) is an energy field that vibrates at a frequency which overlays the physical body's cellular level life force. Spirit is the "glue" that binds together the vibrations of the soul and the physical body.

There is no significant difference between spirit and soul; it is mostly a play on words. The soul may be considered that portion of the Self that resides within the body. The spirit is the portion that resides outside of the physical body.

When you began your process of soul evolution, you started as a memory, nothing more and nothing less than a memory of the Creator. You then set yourself up in search of all the experiences that could possibly occur. Some view this as an evolutionary trap, but it is simply your own plan that brought you to this point in your growth process. No matter what your current circumstances are, you begged, pleaded, cajoled, and did everything in your power to get into this Earth life. You wanted to feel. You wanted to experience. You wanted to learn.

One of the facets of this dimension you learn most about is the emotions. Women are generally more open and free with experiencing their emotions, but learning to deal with them is just as important for men, perhaps more so. Emotions are so important because as the Shift approaches, everyone will be opening to their inner Truth and becoming more aligned with the Earth, the universe, and all dimensions.

The Oversoul

Each soul is part of an Oversoul. The Oversoul consists of a large number of souls. Imagine the soul being a terminal tied into a huge computer. This massive computer has many terminals, and ordinarily you see only what is on your own terminal. The Oversoul is your totality, your Truth, all that you are. It is your essence. Between you and the Oversoul is your higher self. Your soul is an aspect of your higher self, which, in turn, is an aspect of the Oversoul.

An aspect is another part of your soul energy and can be seen as a new program that comes to you every six to eight years. It is a part of your total essence; a new direction for your soul growth or evolution, a new set of experiences for you to undergo. The aspect merges very gently into your third-dimensional Self. Sometimes you can actually have a double aspect actively working at the same time in the same body! Although this may cause confusion in the soul, usually an agreement has been made between the aspects of the souls prior to birth.

Literally thousands of souls in the Oversoul exist in different dimensions, in different universes, and in different planetary systems. In order to align yourself to your Oversoul, you must align your consciousness and energy to the dimensional aspects of your own soul family, which consists of approximately six to nine entities. You may also have other aspects of yourself existing somewhere else on this planet. Through the energy of love, the alignment is seen as evolving to the clarity that there is no separation at all.

Genderless Soul

The soul is neither male nor female. A soul may have an inclination to be male or female in a particular incarnation, but it will vibrate with whichever energy is more natural to it.

The energy field of the soul accounts for 30 to 40 percent of the physical body's energy field, with most of that soul's energy being outside the body. If the soul's energy in a male body had about 75 percent female vibration, that male could have more of a feminine inclination.

Soul Evolution

There are no shortcuts, my friends. The only reason that you are here is that you have chosen to go down this path. The soul experiences so that it can evolve. The physical body is a vehicle for the soul to experience physical sensation. In the higher dimensions, sensations are basically a memory. We know about it. We see it in vibrations, sound, and frequencies—what you call "geometry."

The soul uses the Third Dimension to evolve, through positives and negatives, yin and yang, polarity or duality. As part of the growth process, the soul realizes that the duality it has been trying to balance in this dimension is all an illusion. That realization is important because it is the process, and each has chosen to experience it. There is no shortcut to soul evolution.

Soul Family

Certain groups of souls will bond together in a soul family, for they choose to be your mother, mate, or brother in another incarnation. For the greater part, this family unit will assist each soul member on whatever karmic and/or repeating lessons that the soul wishes to go through. One essence that moves in a higher rate of evolution will progress to higher levels of understanding, while another one choosing to repeat lessons will move along at a slower pace. Although the members evolve at different rates, eventually the gap closes. Members take on incarnations that are necessary to aid their own evolution and that of the other soul members' evolution.

If you are fortunate enough to recognize a soul relative here in this dimension, this is an opportunity to understand why and how to interact with them.

The Death Experience

There comes a point in an incarnation when the soul chooses to leave its physical embodiment. Death may range from a simple leaving of the body during sleep to a violent exit, such as an auto accident. There is also the possibility that a death was planned to assist another human in his or her journey, in which case, both entities gain major growth at the same time. As an evolving entity, the soul's highest journey is to experience all possible realities.

Suppose you are about to have an accident, and there is no chance for survival. Just before impact, your soul leaves the body and finds itself above the scene watching the entire event unfold. The soul does not need to experience the pain associated with this kind of exit.

A calm peace settles over your energy. You concern yourself with the living entities still on Earth. They may be in for some trying lessons, depending on your relationship with them while you were alive. No matter what the relationship was, death definitely takes on a beautiful path for you at this point. You, the ascending soul, will now know what real truth is all about. There is no anger, grudges, or other earthbound emotions to work through. You know all is perfection; all that was in the Third Dimension was how it was supposed to be.

It may surprise you that you don't feel sorry for any of the people left behind. You have no remorse. You recognize that the body is nothing but a thread that you've been using to get around the Third Dimension with. It is absolutely of no use to you any more.

Newly departed souls may stay on the Earth plane for a few days because they want to cajole and console those they left behind. To the latter, I say, "Listen. Listen well." It's not just that you *thought* you heard something. You *did*! They communicate with you. You see, if they could read this book, they would know that you're right there. All they need to do is communicate through their mind's eye. Isn't that great?

In third-dimensional experience, you are a soul. The third-dimensional body isn't really even you; it's simply a vehicle for soul experience. Life is the one thing that you come here to experience, but it also scares you because you become attached to the existence and don't want to let go of it. The death experience is actually more like the birth experience. What you are truly doing is returning home to be with the All That Is.

Questions and Answers

Why do we keep returning to the Earth plane?

KIRAEL: It is impossible to experience all there is to learn in one lifetime. As a soul progresses in the different incarnations, it has the opportunity to complete many experiences each lifetime. The only question remaining is whether it wants to complete an experience in this lifetime or whether it desires to repeat the same circumstances in future incarnations before learning the lesson.

In the planning stages, before we come onto the Earth plane, at what point do we choose our parents? Do we make agreements in the so-called "ethers" with these parents?

KIRAEL: Most agreements are made prior to conception. Conception is a matter of getting the right DNA to combine in the right way.

Let's say that you're ready to incarnate. The first thing you do is consult with your guides, your own personal counselors. Together you decide what you want to work on in this lifetime. You examine your past lives and your incomplete experiences. A plan is developed to create circumstances that best suit what you want to accomplish in the new lifetime.

The next step is to find a birthing channel (mother), and a set of parents who would offer the best possible opportunity for you to fulfill your destiny. Your parents are also looking for a soul to be their child who will aid their growth.

The first place to look is your own Oversoul for any evolving souls that would have the desired qualifications, that are currently in the Third Dimension, and that are in a position to be of service to you. You need to find souls that have already been incarnate for twenty years or so, who are also working on their own plan. If you don't find any such soul in your immediate Oversoul, you may then go to other Oversoul groups.

As a part of the choosing process, you look at their lives and you consult with their Guides to see where they are headed. The Guides will give you the most probable reality, the path those souls will follow, and how each of their lives will interact with yours.

Once you have been conceived by your parents, you will want to try the body on for size. The first fitting is always totally uncomfortable and the urge to get back out of the body is difficult to overcome. Over the nine-month gestation period, while the body is still growing, you move in and out many times in an attempt to align your energy and bring your totality to a complete adjustment. While in there, one of the things you like to do is spring the little legs straight out. Ping! And your mother says, "Oh, it's kicking!" You're not kicking. You're trying to figure out how to maneuver your new limbs while still in the confines of the womb. You're in this warm pool of fluids, all warm and cuddly, but it's cramped and there's nothing you can do about it.

Meanwhile, you're still in contact with your own Guides, and those of your Mom, and sometimes even those of your Dad. Until you have made the final decision to assume this particular life, you can still choose to curtail this incarnation. One way out is stillbirth, where nothing can be attributed to the infant's death, only that it no longer lives. A second way out is crib death. Again, there is no evidence as to the why, only that that it "just happened."

These are often referred to as escape hatches, where the incoming soul had aligned its energy with that of a parent's current life plan, only to find that this particular parent altered its journey to the point where the incoming soul can no longer evolve in the manner desired. For example, the incoming essence had lived a number of lives experiencing wealth and in this incarnation had chosen a parent who was struggling with finances. While this incoming soul is in the fetal stage, the parent working with financial burdens suddenly changes its life plan by winning the lottery, thus moving to a whole new lesson plan. This situation no longer works for the incoming entity, hence the escape hatch.

Suppose you have reached the age of two, and suddenly you are "tragically" killed in a traffic accident. Your parents might ask, "If there is a God, why would He do this?" Let me assure you, God didn't make it happen, yet God definitely allowed the exploration of that form of soul evolution for you and your parents. Try to avoid judgment at this point, for there has been an agreement between both the souls of the parents and soul of the child wherein all wanted to go through this type of experience for their own evolution.

Often, one of the players is referred to as an "in-service soul," an entity committed to be in service. A baby who dies in the crib has provided the parents with the necessary experience of losing a baby. All evolved souls have probably already done this work, so before you get too miffed with the Creator, try to understand the total picture.

Anyway, let's assume that you have chosen a body to begin your evolutionary journey. You don't take complete and total physical possession of the body until your actual birth. The body is already yours, of course, but you don't stay in it all the time. Even after you're born, you don't stay in the body all the time. This is one of the reasons that the little ones sleep so much. In truth, they are still journeying back and forth.

You mentioned that the soul goes in and out of the body while it is in the womb. Well, how does this affect abortions?

KIRAEL: That's all part of the plan, my friend. That's why I wanted to emphasize that you are in and out of the body while in the womb. There are a number of souls who incarnate just for that purpose. Let's say a young woman wants to have an abortion as part of her life experience. This is something that she planned "up there." So she looks in her own soul family for a volunteer. I know it sounds frivolous but that's exactly what happens. The volunteer soul enters and is in and out during the pregnancy. After the abortion, the soul gets to go back home again, and the young woman is thankful for that soul's help.

When you're planning your life, if the issues you want to deal with are health problems, would you pick a parent who has the DNA for a particular disease?

KIRAEL: Yes, you would attempt to pick parents who have the potential for that illness within their DNA coding. However, your parents do not have to be pre-coded; if it is your journey to have poor health, you are going to succeed. Quite often you pick the parents and not a particular disease such as tuberculosis. You just pick a life where you are going to have a set of circumstances that will teach you what it is like not to be in full strength of the third-dimensional body. So if it turns out that this parent is very susceptible, and way down deep, the genes have a tendency toward polio or whatever ailment is needed, then it will be in the DNA. You bring in everything that you need, and you can also pick out from a parent whatever you need. This explains why sometimes, when you look at a child, the parents do not have one of the symptoms whatsoever, yet the child has it. And the doctor says, "Well, I don't understand because it's supposed to be hereditary." Well, guess what? The child did get it from the parents, but the doctors might have to dig a lot deeper than they thought. This is how you make the whole thing work out.

Take a disease like epilepsy, for instance. Epilepsy is a very profound example of someone trying to stay and go at the same time, since consciousness is frequently disrupted. Maybe the higher self strives to retain contact, but the seizure gives you a temporary opportunity to go "home."

The seizure is based on the carbon-based molecular and electrical systems and the work of certain light beings who take control of the body during an episode. Third-dimensionally, the individual consciousness has left and is unaware of the passage of time. It could be in five different universes simultaneously.

Medication may help until the "I AM" Self ultimately chooses when you go out. You can get the body to produce, through meditation, the equivalent of what your medication is doing. Look at it this way: Pills are produced by thought. In order for someone to arrive at the thought to create the pill, the body must have been able to produce a similar substance.

Please understand that life is one giant illusionary play, more like a dream. In this dream, you are able to change and maneuver any part. It's your journey. Like all else in your movie (dream), you script it, choose the actors, and plan your own starring role. Have fun with it.

I know one soul who had just completed a life where she was a beggar. That soul learned all that she needed to learn and never had to be a beggar again. The parents she picked in the next life are anything but beggars, so of course the experience is totally different. Though the situation may differ, the traumas can seem every bit as hard as those of other lives. You see, when you are in the experience, you always play it out to the point where the experience is fully assimilated and does not need to be repeated. Get the idea?

Can you tell us something about patients who are in a coma?

KIRAEL: Comas are not as they appear. For the most part, those in this level of consciousness are processing more information than so-called conscious people. Often this state of awareness is used to allow the physical body the chance to heal uninterrupted, while allowing the higher essence to continue its path of choice.

Please remember that people in comas can hear everything around them. Even though the essence is astral traveling, the brain stores the information to be replayed upon its return. So if you know people in this situation, talk to them. Keep them up to date on current events, and most of all, let them feel your love, for love is the single most important thread that links them to this reality.

When the being is ready to return to this reality and resume life in the Third Dimension, he or she will leave all the accumulated experiences veiled, for placing all this information into linear format is most often too difficult.

Would you speak on the subject of suicides?

KIRAEL: Because of the vast compression of the energy on Earth, this is a subject that is becoming increasingly important.

Souls must experience everything throughout their different incarnations, including suicide. This is something usually done in the early stages of soul development, that is, as a young soul, and any attempt to repeat the experience will bring the absolute worst plan that a soul can encounter.

In the case of a repeated suicide, the returning soul is met by Master Guides who review what happened. Let's try and save anyone reading this material the sadness of this. It is commonly believed that in this situation you will be allowed to repeat the life circumstances up to and including the exact point of death. The real question is how many times your soul has experienced this moment. If it doesn't sound fun, that's because it's not. Therefore, the next time you hear of someone contemplating suicide, please share this with them and hopefully save them a repeat incarnation along with all the horrors that caused the situation.

The next time you are confronted by someone threatening suicide, you might share the following with that person:

> "If it is not in your plan and you should be so unfortunate as to succeed, here's what will happen. Immediately upon success, you will meet with all your guides. The first thing they will want you to understand is that you have made a dreadful error and

that suicide was not the answer. More importantly, while in life review, you will learn that, in the next life, you will reach the exact same point and hopefully you will choose differently, for the situation will be repeated indefinitely until you do."

Simply put, when you choose suicide, you will recreate the exact same set of experiences in another life, including exactly what led up to the suicide.

How far can the soul travel while still incarnate?

KIRAEL: When you are incarnate, you can only get a certain distance from your body. Usually you are not permitted outside the galactic dimension. Incarnation on other planes, such as on Pleiades, Sirius, or Andromeda, does not have the same restrictions. Earth incarnations explore the younger aspects of the soul, so "reality jumping" is restricted.

Will you address the events that occur immediately after a person joins the light?

KIRAEL: First, you will be attracted to a beautiful light. The light is the warmest, most enticing of anything you can imagine. Take the best experience of your entire lifetime and amplify it about a hundred thousand times. That's the feeling you will experience as you approach the Christ Light.

Once you are accustomed to the Light, you will encounter your friends and family, mainly those that have passed away. They are there to make your transition as smooth as possible and to see that you suffer no fear. After a period of time with your friends, you begin your life review. This is by far the most exciting process because you can observe every experience of the immediate past life while actually learning from it. Throughout this time, your Guides will help you to move in and out of scenes to get the clearest picture and to recognize the possibilities that you may have missed so that you can start to build your experience for the next incarnation.

Is there some sort of grading system for the life review?

KIRAEL: The only criterion of importance during the review is the extent of your soul's evolution. Each lifetime on Earth moves you closer to completion. All the experiences in your life plan will to some degree have been played out. This is why it is so important to be as complete as possible in each experience. You determine the degree of soul evolution. No particular entity will be as harsh a grader as Self.

The life review is one of the most important parts of a soul's journey. It is here where you examine your last incarnation in its entirety and begin composing future lives. The possibilities are endless. The review is exciting. You get to re-experience every second of that life. You can understand why you chose to act or react to the many situations you've experienced. As to actions that you knew were wrong even at the time they were happening, absolutely nothing you do is without learning. During the review, you will see the real reason for the incident and the insight will be worth the lesson. No matter how hard the lesson, remember that it was all part of your master plan.

The review has no real measurable time; you may take as long as you wish to go back over and over the scenes of a life. Sometimes the repeating of the review helps establish the next life pattern. Other times, you can learn just by watching.

Can we get in touch with those we leave behind?

KIRAEL: The answer is an absolute "yes." But will those that are left behind listen? Most humans are not prepared to hear when a spirit speaks to them. Even when they do listen, it usually scares the heck right out of them.

I have heard you speak about soul families before. Could you elaborate?

KIRAEL: Oftentimes, the soul family will congregate close to each other while journeying through the Third Dimension. You may be surprised at how that so-called "best friend" is much more than a friend. Physical family members are often of the same soul family, but it is definitely not a rule.

What makes this really interesting is that in a particular life, one who is a son or daughter in this lifetime may very well be an older soul than the parent in the realities of the soul family. Thus, with this thought in mind, you may have a higher understanding of your relationships with other family members.

Can you talk about ghosts or the non-physical beings roaming around Earth?

KIRAEL: For clarity, let's assume we are talking only of a lost soul and not of a malevolent soul who is intentionally trying to disrupt lives. In the case of the latter, get professional help. A soul usually becomes Earthbound or, as most would say, a "ghost." This is usually because after the funeral process, rather than ascend into the awaiting Light, the departing soul extends its stay and loses sight of the Light. This could happen when the grieving mourners wail at the top of their lungs for the departed. The departed soul may want so badly to be of service, that it will try to extend its time of exit. When this happens, confusion then sets in as the soul becomes used to the Earth's energy and loses interest in moving on. It may reach a point where it will need divine intervention to find its path. This is why there is a need for ghost "healers" on this dimension. Actually, you can easily remove a soul from a residence or business if you can just get past the fear. All you have to do is locate the lost soul, communicate with it, and re-acquaint it with the Light. The lost soul will move so fast into the Light that you normally don't have a chance to say good-bye.

How long can an Earth ghost remain on Earth?

KIRAEL: Ghosts have no idea of time. They can be on the Earth plane for several hundred years and hardly even know it because they don't have an internal clock. They're just here.

In referring to energy patterns as ghosts, remember that this is simply the pattern of an evolving soul, destined to complete a particular personification. Although the chance of confusion is high, there is always a reason for its presence. In understanding this, it becomes evident that being of service to this entity is in alignment with the Light. It is a matter of helping the entity to find the Light or just relocating it to a space of love to complete its journey.

Ghosts aren't here to hurt anyone. Most of them are just confused because they are seeking the light that was first shown to them at the death experience. Not connecting with this light source, ghosts begin to wander, trying to remember the path home. Compassion is in order, for the thought of being lost for that length of time is quite disconcerting.

The next time you hear of a ghost in someone's house, try to communicate with its essence. Maybe you could create a light for it to enter into. That is better than doing nothing at all.

Can anyone go directly to the Angelic Realm, or is there a place of training?

KIRAEL: Interesting question for, in fact, most are involved in training for the Angelic Realm. Angels play an important role in the order of ascension. There are those of the Angelic Realm who have no need to process a human life. To attain this level, one must have understood and resolved the vast number of issues surrounding all life forms.

When the cycles of understanding are completed on the third-dimensional level, a normal passage into an angelic presence is somewhat standard. There are many reasons for this, yet probably the most important is because one can use the vast number of lessons learned in order to be of service to all those who are still ascending.

In trying to place the reality of the Angelic Realm in a linear space, it may be best to say that angels are central to evolution, as their essence on this plane can work miracles in any and all possible guardianships.

How do we work with our guides?

KIRAEL: The first and surely the most important thing to remember about working with Guides is that they are not called "Doers," they are called "Guides." It is not their purpose to do for you. However, if you learn to call on them and, more importantly, to listen to the messages sent back, the walk through this journey becomes a beautiful experience.

So open your hearts, my friends. Open your hearts wide. Within your heart lie all the answers for which you are looking. You will grow. Your prosperity, your happiness, your dreams, all that you are trying so hard to attain, can be yours. If you look within, you will see that attainment has already been achieved. So listen to your hearts, my friends. Open up, and you will see that, for all the questions you have, you already have the answers. Society has conditioned or programmed you to look outside of self for truth. In reality, Truth lies within.

Enjoy all that you are doing. Love what you are doing. It is all your creation. You must get to the point of understanding that all that is happening around you is your own creation. If you do not like what you are doing, then learn the lesson and change it. It is that simple. It is time to look at your truth. If you look inside, you can see the light. You can also help your brothers and sisters to move forward, to heal as you heal, to guide as you will guide.

This third-dimensional aspect that we call "self" is just an aspect of your totality, one small part of the whole. You are multi-dimensional beings. Learn to experience all of your dimensions in this lifetime and your soul will evolve to a higher state of consciousness.

Let me share a manner of prayer that has helped many to reach the desired results of their journey:

> *Allow yourself to relax while breathing deeply.*
> *Begin to feel the presence of a beautiful light surrounding your body.*
>
> *Call on the Creator to hear your words.*
>
> *In that moment, we often fail to recognize the beauty that surrounds us. So first, take a moment to thank all your Guides, being thankful for the grand things that have happened in your life.*
>
> *Secondly, ask that the signposts put before you on a daily basis be clear, for in this, you will do your best to carry out this daily adventure to the highest level possible.*

·6·

The Galactic Brotherhood Connection

UPDATE FROM KIRAEL

KIRAEL: I want to tell We the People in this chapter that, when I first wrote this book, I put a whole lot in there about the galactics. And the first person, the first editor that got ahold of it, took a lot of that stuff out. But what I figured out later on, it was because we needed to focus on you, We the People. And so, I add to this chapter this day: If you have the heart strength to read what I made them leave in there, you will know why they might have taken some of the other stuff out, because maybe it was just too noisy at the time.

But let me say this to you so clearly: So many of me friends have written about the galactic world, and don't you know, they've said, "Oh, the galactics are going to land on the White House lawn on such and such a date." And they got everybody all excited about it. And then, of course, it didn't land on the White House lawn. And so they became discouraged and all of the people that read their work became discouraged.

But here is what I tell you: You are one star system inside just your Milky Way Galaxy, not the cosmos; you are one star sun star system amongst 400 billion others. Now, if you think that the Creator had nothing better to do than to focus everything it had on one little planet, you might be in for a wee surprise, because many of you reading this work are going to remember living in other worlds. Some of them may have been the world of Lemuria right here on this planet, some 50,000 years ago. Others of you may have come from other star systems to get here.

And I can bet you on this little statement here: All of you reading this book are at least a conglomerate of other life forms, because when the Creator designed you called the human, it took a little piece of the best of everything and made you look just like this. Go look in the mirror. You will see what the Creator thought was the best of all worlds, because, don't you know, you are one of the late-earliest bloomers that we have.

So, your galactic friends. What I am about to say to you will not be popular in the galactic world, but I'll say it anyway: It is as though right now the galactic world wants to come down onto your planet and just give you everything that they know. But they've decided to let you find out for yourself. And so, they sneak it into you a little bit at a time.

You know this thing that you have called a computer? You want to guess where it came from? It didn't come from your Earth plane, my friends. You weren't ready for it. But the galactics sneaked it in. So, they love you beyond your wildest dreams. They're just tired of every time they have a little warble in one of their engines and you get to look at them, they are just tired of you trying to shoot at them. So stop shooting at them.

The next time you see one in the sky — now listen to me, especially if one of you We the People live in a place called Sedona, Arizona, where they fly around the skies something unbelievable. But the next time you see one, don't jump up and down in joy and scream and holler. You remember that thing in the other chapter where I said put those little particles together? Well, you got darn near enough photon energy to do it right now. I put out a little chart every month, every month that tells you how much is available to you.

So the next time you're standing up on the Bell Rock or if you are standing on Diamond Head, or if you are standing on Mount Fuji, and you see one of those black shapes in the sky, don't jump and down. Put your particles together; send it love. It will be so honored, it just might drop out of the sky and say hello to you.

I think it is time that we close the gap between that world and yours. You are going to have to do it in love because that is the only thing that they know. The galactics are amongst you, some of them are living next door to you. But know this: They are all coming awake, and they are loving what they are seeing, because We the People are reading these books—this book in particular.

●●●

KIRAEL: This may be a perfect time for some page skipping for those who are still struggling with the possibility of other life forms from distant galaxies.

This chapter is not intended to prove whether they exist or not but to discuss how to interact with them at the appropriate time. In the Shift, many from different realities will have active roles, and none shall be greater than this. We will start by exposing a fact that makes all possibilities realistic and will complete this with a true clarity of why cover-ups are no longer of importance.

Your sun is one of 100 billion stars in the galaxy with planets revolving around it, and the Hubble Space Telescope has shown that this galaxy is only one of over 200 billion galaxies. Imagine the possibilities. Do you still think Earth might be the only one out there with living, evolving beings? I think it would be quite arrogant to think you are the only ones. Can you believe that the Creator said, "Yes, with all this space, I'm just going to make life on this one little planet"? Still, there are those out there who do not want to believe it. They believe that humanity is all there is.

Your galactic brothers and sisters, known collectively as the Galactic Brotherhood, are here to help prepare you for the Shift. For the most part, you haven't been able to detect them yet, but they are already here. Some of the first at the scene were from the system of Sirius. (Sirians and your Earth plane are well matched as far as gravitational forces.) You also have Pleiadians and Andromedans here. And there are many more, but these three in particular are very important to your Earth plane because, when the Shift does come to pass, they will play significant roles in settling the new energies.

ET Cultures—Where Do You Fit In

We are going to talk about what you call "extra-terrestrials," or ET's. They are not thrilled about that name, by the way. Does "extra" mean they are leftovers? Anyway, I will refer to them as "ET's."

Usually when I speak to groups, there are a number of ET's actually in the audience. One evening as we were on the way to a radio station, the medium asked me to be extra kind as the subject was about our galactic neighbors and we wouldn't want to hurt any feelings. In the first place, it would be rather difficult to do that because, as a rule, the ET's are usually somewhat advanced and have learned to deal with this disguise you call "ego." Even the ones acting out a third-dimensional role seem to have a good grasp.

ET's are usually intellectually superior; not that they are smarter, but they are not as veiled as terrestrials. "Veils" are limits placed by the Self, so that when you come to the Earth plane you can enter fully into the experience and learn as many different things as you can. Once you have experienced everything possible, you no longer have to incarnate.

A group of ET's has lived underground undetected by humans for many years on the West coast of America. As Mother Earth begins the Shift, certain parts of the continents will reform. This alien colony is aware that their location is unsafe and has put out a distress signal to their kind in space. This call will be answered. These beings cannot come to the surface because, over their evolution, they have lost the genetic defenses that you have. Simply put, they cannot defend themselves with anything other than love.

Keep a small prayer that the rescue will happen at a time when all can be done in the light, despite the Hollywood fear-based dramas that reduce the chances of a safe and secure rescue. Too much emphasis has been on how best to defeat ET's, but this particular situation may provide you with an opportunity to avoid conflict.

ET's Have Egos

Believe it or not, ET's have egos—not the human kind of ego, but beyond what you understand as ego. They also like to have fun. Once in a while they will pop into view, cruise up beside one of your passenger or military jets, and literally just have fun. The pilots can't tell anybody because if a pilot reports sighting a UFO, he is considered unstable and automatically grounded. If you were a pilot risking the loss of income, would you make this report? That's one of your government's little games, and the ET's love it. Nobody is going to tell on them.

ET Update

A recent development is the appointment of a new council to oversee security in your part of the galaxy. It is made up mainly of Andromedans, whose purpose is to protect and defend, and to ensure the peace and tranquility around your star system.

Sirians bore this responsibility for many years until they entered a Shift similar to the one beginning here. They were seen as an aggressive society. Though the stories of their aggression were not all unfounded, it was a learning process, and, as in all learning, mistakes take place. They have been guardians of Earth for a long period and have just recently handed parts of that responsibility over to the Andromedans. The work they did helped lay the foundation for future groups to become involved without all the turbulence. It was a smooth transition, completed in April 1997.

A major reason for the turnover was the extremely advanced craft used by the Andromedans. Their Alpha-class craft looks much like the orca whale, down to, and including, the colors. The new technology is quite superior in its ability to interact with the Earth's atmosphere. The Alpha-class is one of the most up-to-date in the galaxy. Its most intriguing aspect is "space warp." From the outside, it appears between 4,000 and 6,000 feet across, but the interior appears many times larger. That's right, the inside appears much larger than the outside. This is because they have learned to manipulate space and time just as you will after the Shift.

Another defining quality of the Alpha-class is the way it maneuvers. It takes just one entity to operate the entire ship, simply by focusing energy. The craft also operates without heat, sound, or energy displacement, which makes it undetectable by radar.

Even though Andromedans are very protective, they are also known to be highly intellectual, with extremely advanced brain systems. Despite the efforts of movie producers to depict the ET's as conquerors, you may be assured, this is not the case. They have no desire to be your adversaries; in fact, they are truly here to be of service.

Most UFO activity is not detectable by your technology. If you see a spacecraft in your atmosphere, it may be malfunctioning or choosing to be seen. However, the number of sightings will increase as the Shift nears. The Galactic Brotherhood will, by choice, increase their visibility so that when the time comes to interact with your population, their appearance will be less shocking. Their arrival and ability to assist in the healing of Mother Earth will prove to be most welcome.

On another matter, a recent US Air Force report announced that the UFO that crashed at Roswell in 1947 was, in fact, a hot air balloon manned by crash dummies. Your government spent millions of dollars of your money to come up with this official explanation of one of the most controversial, unexplained phenomena of modern history. I leave you to decide whether it was money well spent.

What I share is the possibility that what truly took place is a craft was captured, and that some of the information obtained would have altered the way the Earth's population had become so dependent on things like fossil fuel and fear-based teachings—things that would surely have threatened the balance of peace and superficial tranquility of life on Earth. For those thinking it is my intention to defame your current financial, political, and social control systems, understand my purpose is only to offer a different perspective so that when the Shift is fully underway, you will begin to know where to look and how to read the signs.

ET's and Earth's Magnetic Grid

Long ago, magnetic grids were put around the planets and moons in your solar system that have molten centers, to allow easy maneuverability for visiting craft from other planetary systems.

You will soon discover that in the last Shift, the exterior of Earth actually rotated, but the grid didn't. This explains why galactic visitors often have a difficult time approaching Earth, and why, for the most part, they stay well outside the gravitational pull of the planet. In addition, they find certain places on this planet difficult to live in, while other locations just feel better.

Things to Come—A Reality Check

There is much wild speculation about government cover-ups when it comes to our galactic brethren, and the scary part is, most of it is true. What is shared is for you to ponder, remembering that always it is a matter of letting your heart choose.

Newly sworn-in presidents of the United States are briefed on closely guarded secrets that are felt to be too alarming for the general population to know. As to how detailed this presentation is, only a handful of people really know, yet it is said that the President is given two options. Option 1 is to reveal this material, of course, raising the possibility of disastrous ramifications that could weaken the government. Option 2 is to continue the cover-up at an enormous cost, to keep information that supposedly does not exist from the very people who are paying for the cover-up.

In the post-Shift era, those charged with revealing this information will hold nothing back, seeing that only Truth will serve to allow the heart to resonate with what humanity needs to know.

In conclusion, let me reiterate that the ET's are on your side, no matter how Hollywood depicts them. They are here to assist all in making the best possible transition into the new energy. With all the technology, if they meant you harm, there would be nothing you could do to resist. So treat them well, for they are only welcoming you back to the Alliance.

Question and Answers

How did the entities in the Galactic Brotherhood become members?

KIRAEL: First and foremost, by choice. After thousands of years, as measured here on Earth, they came to a collective understanding that life could be lived through love as opposed to fear. You see, fear keeps evolving entities from aligning.

Are there carbon-based (human) Galactic Brotherhood members on this Earth plane?

KIRAEL: Yes, there are many. Many have chosen human form so they can help this planet prepare for the Shift. They have interrupted their current plan so as to be accepted in your reality. Some of them still have the veil surrounding them and don't even remember who they are. This could mean you!

Are members of the Galactic Brotherhood and galactic councils the same entities as those from as far back as Lemuria?

KIRAEL: There are definitely entities still working within the councils who have remnant energy dating back to Lemuria and other lost societies. They are some of the highest sources of guidance on the journey.

Is the Galactic Brotherhood the same as the Galactic Council?

KIRAEL: The Galactic Brotherhood is the collective of all galactic energy. The Galactic Council has a "leadership role." When I speak of leadership, you automatically see a chain of command. The reality is that there is no superior role. As you know, without the All, nothing can evolve.

Would you expand on the magnetic grids? Why is it important to be able to spot them?

KIRAEL: The magnetic grids hold your planetary system in its orbit while staying in the right rotation, and they can smooth the Earth's transition into the Photon Energy.

It really began to come to light when the Earth underwent Harmonic Convergence. A tiny shift in the Earth's axis had not been accompanied by a shift in the grid. Without full alignment, the landing calculations used by ET's for thousands of years had to be altered. This kind of occurrence hampers the ET's ability to be of service in your pre-Shift awareness. The grids must be fixed so that the ET's can again use this valuable tool. Don't lose faith. Everyone is working on it.

The reason for all the activity in your skies at this particular time and for ET's showing themselves is that they feel they can be a bit more visible. They are learning how important it is to help as many as possible who want to move through this Shift.

How do I know if I'm located in a grid area? What do I do when I locate these areas? How can I help in straightening out the grid lines?

KIRAEL: It is not a matter of straightening the grid lines but of identifying how far off they are. Once you do that, maybe there is something that the ET's can do. I have found from a little higher source that through the simple act of chanting "Om," you can cause a vibration that helps all the powers that are currently working on this project. Even if by that effort you are not able to completely align the grid, that will be of assistance. Through Truth, you can be sure of locating how far off they are, and through the Om process, can relay that information to the ET's. Then they may be able to adjust their frequencies to match up with it. The problem is that Earth is already in the Shift. Each time we think we've come closer to understanding the grid, it seems to move. However, we know that this motion can be corrected.

Recently, the Hyakutake comet passed near Earth. As it was passing, scientists observed that it seemed to be emitting X-rays. Many scientists say that this is impossible because a comet is a cold ball of ice and dust. They haven't really been able to come up with a good explanation. Was it emitting X-rays? If so, what is the significance of this?

KIRAEL: The comet was not emitting X-rays, but "free rays." Another planetary system it passed placed a transmitter in it, and it sends knowledge back as it travels. The transmissions are called "free rays" because anyone can tap in. It has already passed you and your Earth society. Scientists have already collected the data but have not yet figured out how to decipher it.

Do Hyakutake's free rays have anything to do with ET councils?

KIRAEL: ET councils or galactic councils have access to it and they can add information to it. Back in the mid-1700s, one of the Brotherhoods injected false information into the free ray. That impacted Earth and got a couple of your scientists on a terrible path. The Sirians worked hard to sweep that information out of the free ray. However, most of the ET councils are above all that and don't have anything to do with free rays.

You've mentioned that the Andromedans are acting as a security force or serving in a security capacity for our planet. If the Andromedans, Pleiadians, Sirians, and all the other galactic entities are so much more advanced, why are many of them still confrontational? I don't understand how beings so evolved could get into a confrontational situation where they could have wiped each other out.

KIRAEL: Three or four blocks from here, a gang of youths is sitting around with bandannas wrapped around their heads. They have no remorse about murdering a fellow being, yet they are just as advanced in this society as you are. Would you stick a knife in someone else? Not likely. For some time to come, you're going to have these renegades. Renegades gather forces; weakness feeds on weakness.

Remember also that, like you, ETs have had to evolve, and in the past, there was plenty of room for errors. Now, those who are able to cross dimensions and galaxies have the understanding of Love and what it takes to reach a level of pure Truth, Trust and Passion.

Andromedans have chosen a protector role because, while other groups worked on perfecting many other forms of evolution, Andromedans perfected travel. Their level of evolution is by far the highest, and there is little that could make you feel more secure.

If all of us here have intergalactic connections, some or all of us are aspects of galactic entities, presences, or energies. What can we do to strengthen our memories of these aspects?

KIRAEL: There is not much you can really do in the Third Dimension. It is not so much the arrival as it is the journey you choose to get there. When you enter the Third Dimension, your veil is usually so complete that you choose to separate from all other realities, including galactic realities. Only when you begin to relate to the possibilities does it begin to resonate deep within you that the connection is there.

Another society not so far removed is the dolphin community. They exist in this dimension, yet they don't limit their reality to the veiled experiences of human.

Dolphins operate on up to 100 percent of their brain capacity, while the human population of Earth uses between 8 and 10 percent of theirs. It would seem that the dolphin species might feel quite superior. This is not the case; in fact, they spend a good deal of their time showing that through love.

Humanity needs not be limited to just the five senses. I suggest that those of you having access to these beautiful creatures try to communicate with them. This is not as hard as you may think. Simply start using mind transfer. You will find it easier with an entity using 100 percent of its brain than with almost any other living being. Try it.

After the Shift, the real interaction will begin, and I'll let them explain why they have so generously allowed themselves to be captured and held in captivity. You will be quite surprised, but for now, just remember that they are aligned to the Shift and will be of great service in creating a bridge between the ET and human entities.

Are there other species similar to us spiritually?

KIRAEL: Many. The different levels are vast, yet all civilized worlds understand that spiritual evolution is the real truth. The search for the Source is not confined to the Third Dimension or carbon-based evolution. It is shared by any soul-driven entity wishing to understand the "I AM." Each civilization is working on all four bodies in one form or another, so to judge a civilization's level of spirituality may not be fair to evolution.

Can you tell me what system the writers for the "Star Wars" series movies were from?

KIRAEL: Sirius, but they did not do the actual writing. They were invited to assist on this particular project. Their input is evident, as the craft you see are exact replicas of the Sirian Delta-class. The writers listened extremely well in that the way they maneuvered was excellent. Not only that, but many of the characters were true to form. The entire first movie was in fact based on a true story that happened in a reality quite close to yours. Like so many of your superstars acting out a third-dimensional role, the one who directed this will one day receive some sort of a humanitarian award. Eventually all will discover that he really isn't even human after all.

As stated, many of you are really not from this planet. For instance, a basketball player who can fly through the air and do things seemingly inhuman will one day admit his true origin. Many, many will become aware that if someone seems different, it's probably because they are ET. Oh, how much fun it will be at Shift-time, when they all begin to expose their true identities.

Two nights in a row, I have had dreams that the coming of UFOs is imminent.

KIRAEL: Yes, it is so, and you are not alone. For many, the dreams are going to come in greater frequency and with much clarity. This is one way for the Galactic Brotherhood to begin to align with their entities here on Earth. They are trying to get you all used to the way they look and act so that the population will not go into panic when they begin to manifest.

What times do we look for them and which nights?

KIRAEL: The logical time to see them is in the night sky, preferably in the early morning hours, when there is less static or interference. The sun's powerful rays affect the magnetic grid, so they are seldom visible during daylight hours.

Unusually high levels of volcanic activity indicate that the Earth is vibrating at a higher pitch, causing a shift in energies. This type of Earth shift causes energy to rise, which sometimes disrupts the energy patterns used to cloak a craft. Bright objects also help to conceal spacecraft. Since the full moon brings in the strongest essence of the grid pattern, the craft are less visible during that time.

Sometimes they assume the appearance of a cloud formation. This is not one of their best tricks, however, because they often have to break formation and they get caught.

There was a time when an armada from Andromeda was within your atmosphere. Actually, they were on a training mission. These types of missions are quite common; they like to keep in practice. A standing joke among them is the saying that they aren't here to protect you, but to protect themselves from you. Anyway, as they flew over Hawaii, your radar system found them, and immediately the whole of your military went to something called "Defcon 3."

With jets scrambling and launch site doors opening, they figured it was an appropriate time to disappear.

I have seen what I call a "ship" in the south-southeastern area of the sky. Sometimes it moves. When I look at it with the naked eye, it vibrates green, red, blue, and white. I have looked at it with binoculars and it vibrates like a scrambling worm in the sky. I have watched it for hours and hours. The constellations move throughout the sky in these hours, but this particular object does not move. It calls to me every time it's out there. Can you explain what this might be?

KIRAEL: Of course. This is an unmanned listening post, set up by the Andromedans, out about 2,000 light years. Although they will be increasingly evident to people, someone standing right beside you could be unable to see them. It all depends on what vibration you resonate.

I read somewhere that a group of ET's was attempting to enter Earth so they could devour humans to get the love element of their DNA strands.

KIRAEL: I cannot think of any extraterrestrial that does not have the love aspect. Anyway, they would approach you as individuals working in the attempt to achieve love. Ironically, most of you do not really know what love is about. Sorry, but it is true. You are attempting to learn love. Nobody here really understands love, so I cannot imagine why extra-terrestrials would come down here and try to sap it from your DNA.

One of the major things you are here to do is to understand your emotional system. The emotional body is the number one element of the four-body system, not the physical body. Those of you who struggle with your emotions, who keep pent-up emotions, or who rely on your lack of emotions to get you through this lifetime are quite possibly wasting a lifetime!

In your four-body system, you are here to learn the emotional aspects of Self. Once you learn to ignite the emotional centers, then the love essence becomes a reality. If you were to understand this, we could end this whole conversation right here. You are here to learn what love is and to experience love.

The subject of abduction brings up fear in many people. In truth, it cannot be stated that this type of interaction has never taken place. There have obviously been many visitors to your planet and not all of them were as fully evolved as those currently in service. For a time, the energies coming in contact with Earth were highly evolved in the mastery of mind but lacked balance in the other systems such as emotions. There was even a belief amongst them that, somehow, they could actually take a shortcut in evolving by using the genes harvested from the more emotional Earth beings. It did not take long for them to discover that ascension is a complete journey and that there is no such thing as a shortcut.

Which ET's occupied Earth during Lemurian times?

KIRAEL: The Lemurian culture was predominantly of Pleiadian understanding, whereas the Atlantean was of Sirian vibration. In the next chapter, the connection between these two vibrations show how humanity began to work with fear, so be prepared for a clarity that will raise many questions and challenge many belief systems.

You mentioned that whales were being signaled by the Hale-Bopp comet. If whales are keepers of information, why do they need to be signaled?

KIRAEL: The whales were being told that it was time to release the information. Hale-Bopp has many implications; one is that it is the alarm clock for the whale population.

Like all the great comets, each has a bearing on how history will be shaped. They are used as coordination points for aligning planetary events. ET's use these events to cover up their activities, but with the technology now available to you, their presence is often detected, hence all the controversy over Hale-Bopp and why it was studied so closely.

How is Hale-Bopp related to the Christ Consciousness and to the ET's?

KIRAEL: Christ was in contact with the Galactic Brotherhood. The Christ Consciousness knew that the Great Pyramid and the Sphinx were all galactic. The people from the Egyptian times were told what to write and that they were to leave out flying people. However, you still see some remnants on the walls.

The Christ Energy will be here at the same time as the extra-terrestrials. This is the truth of your Creator Energy. Not only will you be joined by the so-called extra-terrestrials but also by the Christ Energy. At the time of the Shift, many of the Great Masters will also join you, for it is in their knowingness that you will receive all the guidance you need.

The relationship between the comet and the ET's does not have much to do with Hale-Bopp itself but with the energy behind it. In Hale-Bopp's "cargo hold" were literally hundreds of spacecraft. When hundreds of craft—bigger than anything you have ever seen—descend upon your Earth, it is going to be your wake-up call.

What is the real meaning of the crop circles?

KIRAEL: They are patterns of communication, with multiple messages for not only Earth beings but also for many other life forms observing the Shift.

The earlier displays were to verify the evolutionary track that Earth is on. The latest are complex diagrams analogous to the restructuring of particles for developing patterns such as that of DNA.

[Kirael is being shown a photograph.] What does this circle signify?

KIRAEL: There are a number of meanings, yet there is one of particular interest that refers to "ten years after the arrival of the darkened times on this planet." It concerns a time yet to come. This process is referred to as "doctorian" and the possible make-up of a society similar to the ancient civilization of Mu. This is a period well documented in the halls of the Great Pyramids both in Egypt and on Mars.

Signs within this picture indicate that this Great Shift comes soon after the new millennium presents itself. The symbols in the design provide the scientist with the opportunity to begin a dialog with energies not of this dimension. I will discuss dimensional transition in a future book. Humanity is missing awesome opportunities for understanding by ignoring the crop circle phenomenon.

Since humans do not have a predator, did Mother Nature create viruses to keep the population down?

KIRAEL: Let us not pick on Mother Nature. Many of your viruses come from space, and unfortunately, almost as many have been created by humans as an attempt to fix something else.

Most inoculations are, in fact, strains of the disease itself, and things have been created that have literally gotten out of control. Conspiracies have led to governments holding back cures of diseases such as syphilis so they could see the results of no treatment. There was no reason for people to suffer like this. After the Shift, games and cover-ups will no longer be needed.

How are ET's preparing for this major Shift?

KIRAEL: Recently a group of ET's intervened quickly and decisively regarding a secret project called Project Boom Box, which placed a receiver just off the Hawaiian Islands and a sending unit just off the West Coast of the mainland. A sound wave was then to travel the distance of approximately 2,500 miles between these two places, to allow researchers to measure the temperature at the bottom of the ocean.

Now imagine the power of the sound wave it would take to do this. This high-powered signal would have killed the fish population for miles around the transmitter. And if you think that sounds bad, what would it have done to the whales and dolphins with their high sensory capabilities? Imagine the impact of an intense sound wave on them.

They not only called for help, they received it. A craft not of Earth origin sent three bursts of energy into the Earth's atmosphere. The first warned the life forms in the area of the ship carrying the components of this device. The second sheared the cables holding the device to the deck of a ship, causing it to fall into one of the deepest parts of the ocean. The third dismantled certain parts of this device to render it irreparable.

Many questions will arise from this part of the work. When checking to see who approved and funded the project, you will come to understand the real meaning of running into a brick wall. Why do

I tell you this? Because projects such as this do exist. It is time for the population to become aware, because the galactic alliance will not always be able to intervene as they did in this case. This bold course of action was highly exceptional, and the Andromedans intend to make sure that this type of direct intervention will not be repeated until the very height of the Shift.

So again, why do I tell you this? Because, my friends, I care.

Where will the ET's fit in after the Shift?

KIRAEL: Get to be their friends in a big hurry because fossil fuels will be of no value to you after the Shift, and they have information about alternatives.

Briefly, the Andromedans, who are now security, will clean up the debris after the Shift. They have technology in their new craft that will remove many things that will be of no value to the Earth plane. The Sirians will use their technology to help the surviving Earth population, and the Pleiadians will probably come in next, to provide spiritual teachings and information on how to work within the councils. Understand that the Galactic Brotherhood will only come in to whatever level they are invited. They cannot surpass that.

Could you explain how we can prepare others and ourselves for the imminent coming of the Galactic Brotherhood?

KIRAEL: First, do not worry. When they come, it will come on such a vast scale that all will literally watch with mouths open. You will be so caught up in the drama that by the time the first wave has shown itself, all will be calm. You will definitely not experience conflict with them. They are not coming to hurt you the way some movies portray. They are coming to assist you when you will need it the most.

You said that some Sirians would return to their ships after the Shift. Are you referring to "ship" as death or an actual Sirian space ship?

KIRAEL: Those of you Sirians who go back to your ship will do so in the actual sense. However, some may not want to return to the physical Earth plane. The answer, my friend, is that, for the most part, those who have direct ties to ET's will elect to return to the crafts to which they belong.

The Andromedans say that on March 23, 1994, all the black holes started to emit a single frequency at the same time. Does that frequency provide a new vehicle for the healing of Earth? Has it provided healing and the movement of the planetary system into the Photon Belt? Is there a way of accessing this frequency?

KIRAEL: You are on the right path, my friend. Although this is not available to you at this time, it is set up to be accessible to you because the mass consciousness has not awakened to it. As the mass consciousness awakens, it will become available.

Recently, every time I meditate, I hear a voice talking to me and answering questions. I am not able to remember what it says. I don't know what the voice is all about. After the question and answer period stops, my body starts to vibrate. My friend says it is a guide, maybe my higher self. Could you give me an explanation?

KIRAEL: You are picking up a death song, a message from a planet that died light years away. Your conscious mind is shutting down because the information doesn't make sense to you. That civilization is trying to tell you how it destroyed its planet, as you are doing on Earth, and how to avoid the same fate for your planet. I am not saying that you have to carry the responsibility of hearing this information, but that if you have the beauty and the love to accept these answers, they will not be a burden to you.

I suggest you try automatic writing. It may lose a little bit in the translation, but you can write it out in English. Listen carefully and capture the words on paper. Give it to anybody within the Inward Healing Center organization. The messages are not so much about the death of a planet, but about the right of life of your planet.

In closing this particular chapter, I hope that clarity prevails. This is not easily attained, for most of the ET involvement is still shrouded in mystery and raises a number of concerns.

It is said that it would take literally light years to reach the closest planetary system. In determining how much conventional fuel it would take, the numbers are staggering, and many might question the viability of space travel. Be assured, our friends from afar have not used fuel like this for literally thousands of years. In their reality, discoveries have certainly moved well past this energy source to propulsion by aligning with energy. By eradicating the constraints of linear mass, they are not limited by the speed of light.

They have already shared much technology with this world, and still remain in hope that the human race will not use it for destructive purposes as in the past.

When the Earth has finally come under the essence of the Shift, you will know that you all need to evolve together, and that your brothers and sisters from far-off realities will prove to be an alliance, willing to share what you have already known for lifetimes. Together, in resonating to the heart and vanquishing the ego, all will begin anew—the evolution to the ONE.

·7·

Earth's Lost Origins

UPDATE FROM KIRAEL

KIRAEL: In this particular chapter of Earth's Lost Origins, I speak some on many different parts of your world, but in here I would like to only remind you of this: Your world has been populated more times than you'll ever know. I get such a kick from it when I hear your scientists discovered someone that lived 18,000 years ago and had tools. I know some that lived 50,000 years ago and had tools that you have yet to invent. They were called Lemurians.

And this is part of what we call the unknown worlds to those of you who must exist from a history written by the victor. You cannot allow those who have not won to write, so you have to take the winner's viewpoint. And the winner is the one who had the most power, and that is usually because they had the most money.

And you see where I am going with this. There are lost origins that only will you find out about them if you have the courage to listen to what we are talking about. Who is "we"? We, the Kryons of the world, the Kiraels of the world, the Gaias of the world, even the Michaels and the beautiful Ronna Hermans, and the Lee Carrolls, and the Pepper Lewises and the Fred Sterlings— all of them are going to tell you about these origins. And, oh, don't you know, sometimes they are going to see it a wee different than the rest. And don't you know? There is a beauty in that, because you get the choice to feel it with your heart.

You say, "Master Kirael, why can't they all see it the same way?" Because we all looked at it in a different time. We all looked at it in a different vibration. You don't think I spent 20 or 30,000 years on one planet, do you? No more than I'll spend 20 or 30,000 years on your Earth. We go, we see, we report what we see. Our heart tells us what to tell you, because, you see, it is all about these societies, these lost societies. They were there for a purpose.

Here is the purpose. For instance, Lemuria: The Creator needed to know if it could take its highest vibration and make it work on a third-dimensional planet. And try as it might, they were just too advanced. And so the Creator went to all of We the People of Lemuria, and he said, "Some of you, I'd like you to go to other parts of the world. And for those of you that we don't choose to go to the other parts of the world, celebrate your hearts out because we are going to bring you back home into our light."

Oh, don't you know, the Lemurians celebrated. But those that were sent out, they were sent out as scouts, so to speak, of a new generation, of a new understanding. And the Creator developed a new being of light. And, oh yes, even since then there have been times where you just weren't ready to do the journey of the Creator, and it's called you home.

There is a time called Atlantis, and the Creator wanted to see what you would do with the highest technology and not how much to do with it or what to do with it, and that was Atlantis. And don't you know, that you are still searching for Atlantis today? You are still searching for the lost continent of Lemuria. Don't search. Find it in your heart. You'll know when you've found it.

Oh, you may travel one day to the islands of Hawaii, and you may step on the mountaintops of Lemuria. Or you may go to a place called Mt. Shasta and feel the love of the very fringes of Lemuria. Or you know what? You just might want one day—think with me now—you might just one day rise up out of your body, let it rest in sleep, and you may just travel wherever you want to go and see the lost societies, knowing they never were lost. They just kept evolving. Here we are today.

●●●

KIRAEL: Lost origins. History is based on facts passed down from one generation to the next. What will be shared in this chapter is based on facts as they are revealed from sources not widely accepted by historians. To admit the existence of places like Lemuria and Atlantis, one must be willing to recognize that the self-imposed veils one has as human are no longer a reason to live life as it was.

History goes back much further than records indicate. Your modern day archaeologists are uncovering artifacts that date back hundreds of thousands of years, which point to ancient but technologically advanced civilizations.

It is the intent of this work to show that humanity has evolved from the so-called "cave man" to a more highly intellectual level of modem humankind many, many times over. This may stretch your thought process, yet it is quite evident that the Earth plane has undergone a number of shifts just as powerful as the one before you now.

The major differences are twofold. First, this Shift will not completely eradicate a whole society. Second, with information like this book, people have time to prepare for this event. Preparation is not about hiding from this Great Shift but about heading into it with a zest for change, allowing the inner self to journey into a whole new millennium.

At a distant point in history, a very high-level society lived on Earth. The beings on Lemuria evolved to a level where very little remained for them to experience. By their own choosing, this highly evolved society made the sacrifice of reducing their DNA structures to allow human evolution the opportunity to master experiences that are still being worked on today.

Because evolution in Lemuria was more advanced than in other parts of Earth, it became clear that adjustments would be needed in order for a different set of experiences to be played out. What follows is undocumented in the history books but will be verified by future archaeological discoveries. When they uncover the archaeological artifacts from Earth, they will find much of the history we are talking about.

There is more evidence available about Atlantis because it is a much more recent culture than is Lemuria. I understand that in late

1998, off the coast of one of the small islands in the Atlantic, divers may have discovered gold canisters containing written records of the Lemuria/Atlantis period. The writers of that time used an ancient language. Currently, archaeologists and governments have many coded languages on file that they do not understand, given to them by the Galactic Brotherhood. When the records are found, they will be decoded almost instantaneously.

There is a lot of information on Atlantis, but we will focus on the period when the population was arriving from the Lemurian continent. As we begin to disclose what was taking place at that time, we leave room for many to question the purpose behind it. Many will be left to ponder the reality of the Earth plane's evolution. What will be seen as possibly the very first shift in consciousness is truly connected to that of the current vibration permeating the Earth today. This will help to demonstrate how it relates to what must take place in the now.

Lemuria: Heaven on Earth

If you overlay a map of the continent of Lemuria on what is now known as the Pacific Ocean, you will see that the Hawaiian Islands are in fact the mountain peaks of Lemuria.

The Lemurians had reached a fifth-dimensional level, one of pure love. They understood the purity of a love essence. For instance, they had no formal system of government but lived in a culture that allowed each person to bring learning to its highest potential. Councils were established to collect information concerning evolution, and their first priority was always the dissemination of all information to the entire population.

The whole basis of society was that of sharing. Never was one to possess knowledge to be better than another. It was considered detrimental to all growth if anyone were left behind on the evolutionary path. Hence, it became a labor of love to help everyone attain the same level.

The spiritualist had a goal in mind—to bring all into the vibration equivalent to that of the Creator, with no single entity left to learn without the complete support of the total. Again, this was done by councils gathering universal knowledge and disseminating it through the appropriate members.

A council consisted of 12 members, and each was assigned a sub-council of 12 that interacted with each member. Each member of this council of 144 had a council of 8 who were responsible for collecting all available data from established entity groups. Any member of any council could be replaced by the simple act of being asked. It was an honor to be replaced by any evolving soul because this proved that the system was intact. The arrangement assured that every being was knowledgeable enough to fill any position, meaning that no one was in a position of authority. Those leaving a position on this so-called "High Council" were rewarded by being allowed to begin work on their ascension.

Let us talk of the Lemurians themselves. First, their brain usage was usually about 90 to 94 percent, allowing them to understand the conversion of mass to energy, and to travel and communicate in ways unrecognizable by today's standards.

They breathed prana through their crown chakras, and their mouths were used predominantly for eating. They would eat only when they wanted to celebrate something, which in their case could have been almost daily. They were always celebrating something, so eating was not as much needed as it was ceremonial. There were no overweight or underweight beings. In fact, they chose how they wanted to be, and created it.

Lemurians would live as long they wished although a lifetime for them was very different from yours. You live multiple lives in order to undergo many types of experience, whereas they crammed them into one lifetime. Lemurians lived between 600 and 700 or more years at a time and probably never chose to do more than three or four of those lifetimes.

Were they carbon-based? I don't think you could call it a "totally carbon-based body" because they had fifth-dimensional energies. For instance, they could disappear and reappear at will, simply by raising and lowering their vibrations. They would reduce their vibration in order to re-experience an aspect of evolution, and then would raise their vibration again. So, lower vibrational essences in Lemuria were very few.

The Creator's Intervention

In a sense, the Lemurians had evolved to a perfect society and were much too advanced for what the Earth had been established to support. Something had to be done to create a framework where souls could evolve from the beginnings of humanity. The Creator's evolutionary plan was to enable new souls to acquire knowledge through learning the totality of each experience. Experiencing every single aspect of the All was in fact the way of evolution. The Creator used the fact that the continent of Lemuria was sinking from the time of its inception to realign the path that the Earth was on. Remember, this was not the only planetary system in the evolutionary process. By bringing the other systems into action, Earth's path could be adjusted and Earth could once again become the schoolhouse of evolution. Most would see this as a backward movement, but, in reality, it was exactly what was needed at the time.

Evolution on Earth would continue in a completely redesigned form, and those on Lemuria were given the conscious choice either to evolve into non-earthly bodies or to move to a new point in time that would greatly regress them.

You may ask, "Why would any entity that had reached this level of ascension be willing to regress to a shell of human existence?" Most importantly, the Creator wanted humanity to continue using the same physical body, not wanting to start over. Remember, the Lemurians only knew love, and if it was in the Creator's plan, then it had to be perfect.

As for the inhabitants of Atlantis, the Creator had instructed the Pleiadian and Sirian extra-terrestrials on how to implement the regression plan. This explains why the ET's are so interested in the outcome of your current Shift.

Lemurians were more purely God-created entities. Atlanteans were almost predominantly from your galaxy but were acting with awareness of the God Energy. Therefore, the galactics are just as much children of God as the Earth beings and entities from Lemuria. They are all God's beings.

This meant that the galactic energies became one segment of your population, while the other segment of your population was directly from the Creator Force. This carbon-based humanoid combination is the human element on your planet to this day. Currently, the galactic energies and those directly from the Creator Force are so intermixed that it is difficult to tell them apart.

The Atlanteans were probably the more interesting of the two stories because of the evolutionary process they went through. They actually evolved out of a form more closely related to the mental, almost machine-like world, which actually supplanted these galactics with light energy patterns, enabling them to begin a new journey of evolution. Then the intermixing of these two streams took thousands of years and produced a society that is now so far advanced in its own reality that it wishes only to be of service to other evolving civilizations. Thus, two different types of energies became one, which began its own ascension.

Reduction of DNA

The first arrivals to what would be recognized as Atlantis were transformed into the new human formation of the evolving species. The first thing they experimented with was the reduction of their brain usage to 8 to 10 percent and the changing of the DNA structure from 12 strands to the current 2 strands. Remember, this was all voluntary. Reversing evolution was the only way to allow souls to experience development and growth.

As you complete the Shift, you will return to the way of the Lemurian Age, which was started very much along the lines of fourth-dimensional energy. It then shifted itself into more of the Fifth Dimension. Today's Shift process marks a complete circle, because you are finally reawakening to your origins here on the Earth plane. The period of Lemuria and Atlantis is a spiral of evolution.

Cellular Memory Reverberations

In the evolutionary context of the Great Shift, Great Masters like Master Jesus have been such an important part of this whole process. This Great Shift was supposed to have taken place at around the time of the Master Jesus' birth/death era. However, because it didn't, Master Jesus has since become one of humanity's major focuses. It is in part because of what happened with Master Jesus and His teachings that ascension is possible. He taught the purity of Love and Healing, but the world was not ready to experience love at its fullest. This, my friends, was a matter of too much light, too much love, so the Shift was delayed 2,000 years.

Why does fear come when we think of a galactic landing? Because this same scenario brought a dramatic reversal of evolution at an earlier point in history. Though it was the master plan of the Creator, Earth beings still carry within their cellular memory the knowing that in some ways the reversal felt improper. So, to this day, seeing a UFO raises that fear deep in the cellular memory, and this will continue until the current body system is raised in vibration.

The reversal was a major Shift in its own right—probably like nothing we will ever see again, yet still it was part of the master plan. Many of the current inhabitants of Earth still have a cellular memory of the great disruption that permeated this mass change. This is why, to this day, many will refuse to accept the coming shift in consciousness, for the memory is too threatening.

The difference this time is that it is not a reversal but a return to the level it once was, so do not be discouraged. Remember that much of this fear is so deep within the cellular memory that it is almost impossible to access. Remember that your society is still fear-based, and that with each move into clarity, all will begin the awakening. Love, my friends, is the answer.

Pyramids

Let us look now to the pyramids of Egypt, and the difference between recorded history and reality. The pyramids are considerably older than the Egyptian Pharaoh era of 6,000 years ago. The watermarks found on the Sphinx prove this. The process is slow, but the scientists are going to determine the true age of the pyramids and will find something really interesting.

The three main pyramids were built eons ago. They match the pyramids on Mars and align with the three stars in the Orion system.

Every one of these pyramids, not just on Earth and Mars but also on Pluto and other planets, was built by advanced civilizations.

Researchers think that the pyramids were built by balancing the blocks one on top of the other. That is not how it happened. They were built using sound tones. In a sense, they were vibrated into existence. The ancient Egyptians were not capable of this. How could a culture that wanted to be entombed with slaves and boats have the technology to construct a pyramid?

The Egyptians, however, did learn how to copy the smaller pyramids. The writings on the pyramids show pictures of spacecraft and people with larger-than-life heads. The pictures are there, but researchers don't reveal them.

The Great Pyramid in Egypt is, even to this day, one of the focal points of your Earth plane. The locations of the Great Pyramids, the one on Mars, and the one on Pluto reveal a galactic connection between the focal points of all three planets, including Earth. Any time the Creator has worked in conjunction with galactic beings and the Angelic Realm, a pyramid is left as an indicator of an inception of special events. This is where it is marked and this is where it should always be. As they branch out, galactic beings need landing places and the Great Pyramid is the focal point. That is why major planets supporting life will have at least a similar, if not identical, focal point.

Recently a new pyramid was discovered that is located off the south tip of the Big Island of Hawaii. It is almost as large as the Great Pyramid and made almost completely of crystals.

The underwater eruptions near the Big Island are caused by ET's trying to remove the volcanic debris because they need the signals that the pyramid emits. Remember, this is also part of Lemuria. Only as time passes will the truth be known as to the importance of the reality of Lemuria.

Both the Great Pyramid of Egypt and the pyramid off the Big Island are at a latitude of 19.5 degrees. If you take the Great Pyramid, the one that is offset just a hair, and the new pyramid at the south point of the Big Island, and you draw a triangle, you will find something fascinating, which I will reveal in a future book.

Whales and Dolphins

One of the final pieces of the puzzle concerning Earth's lost origins is the record keepers, the whales and dolphins. Over the millennia, whales have gathered and stored information about the history of Earth. Most of their information came from what we call the "magnetic resonance fields," that is, those charged by the Earth's crystal base. Mother Earth absorbs and files every thought for possible future use. She puts it into Her crystal base so it can be transmitted back out to whoever is willing to receive it, in this case, to the whales because they have the necessary brain capacity. Most of the history recorded in the crystals of Earth has been "downloaded" into the minds of the whales because the crystals cannot hold it indefinitely. As a rule, crystals can only hold their information for a few hundred years, and as they wear down in the shifting process, there is a potential risk of losing information. Therefore, all information is passed on to the whale population and relayed from generation to generation. Could they, like humans, add or delete knowledge to further their own cause? No, because they have no cause other than alignment with the Creator.

All the information the whales have is available on a-need-to-know basis. You may think that we need to know it all now, but if you, an average third-dimensional, carbon-based person could see what life is like in the Fourth Dimension through the eyes of a whale, you would lose all desire to continue on this current journey. The beauty would be too overwhelming. We have to be careful, which is why I gently reveal this information. If I gave you everything, you would have no reason to continue with evolution, but you would miss all your experiences and all the fun that you are having.

Unlike the whale population, who best resonate with the galactic energy, the dolphin vibrates with the Lemurian essence. With the whales taking care of the records of this dimension on a very mental plane, it has been left to the dolphins to interact with human evolution, and to try to show humans that this insatiable need to use too much of everything will only keep them from the state of harmony. Many dolphins have died so that as teachers they could lead you to the understanding that all could share this planet. However, the vast numbers that die in fishing nets due to your misuse of the oceans show that they have had little success. I say this not to make anyone feel bad but to enlighten all to the plight of this gentle species that loves you very much.

Questions and Answers

Are those who are researching genetic engineering and cloning reincarnations of the Atlanteans? In addition, were they responsible for the DNA reductions back then?

KIRAEL: They are, yet it is important to know why. Though they operated in the light of the Creator then, they still believe that the experience was unfinished because even now they do not understand the truth of the plan. Still, the lessons continue, and many are still trying to understand their part. Patience, my friends, patience.

Could you shed some insight about my desire to travel to Latin America?

KIRAEL: One of the reasons that you are drawn there is because of a past-life connection. During the "exodus," as we call it, from Lemuria to Atlantis in Latin America, South America, and in Central America, there was a society you refer to now as the red man (Indian). Even though they haven't received much credit, they were famous for building healing temples and for practicing what is referred to as "healing touch." These temples were monumental in size, with some so large that they would be measured in acres. One temple actually exceeded 40 acres.

Your archaeologists are now uncovering road systems that supported one of the most diverse trade route systems known to humankind. All this can be found in your more recent science publications.

Now where you are headed and the reason you are being drawn there is your healing abilities. You will discover there is a whole lot more to healing than where to put your fingers. No two healings are ever the same, and often many forms are needed to cure the same individual. When the understanding of the entire four-body system comes into play, healers will move to new and exceptional techniques. You not only have the touch ability; you are ready to start psychic surgery, which is simply moving into the interior of the body with conscious energy.

Can you talk about the information stored in the Great Pyramid?

KIRAEL: You know that researchers have opened up a special chamber in the Great Pyramid, right? Some people think that most of the important information has already been stolen. While robbers may have gotten some of the less important articles, they were not able to resonate to the magnetic material holding the true secrets, the so-called "mysteries of life." Believe that when the time is opportune, the right entity will literally unravel the mass of material that nobody has resonated to at this point. This is information that will be the source of understanding that aligns third-dimensional energy back to the fourth- and fifth-dimensional plan— a plan that will take you into the new millennium and beyond. This is why not just anybody will be able to resonate to it. After the awakening, the masses will be able to understand the contents and will know how to make use of it.

How far back do the Akashic Records go? How old are they?

KIRAEL: These records can be accessed by any energy pattern that exudes the purity of love and intent that the information sought will not undermine or disrupt the life path of any evolving soul. Simply put, the records are more for those evolved entities who are closing out their existence in moving from one level to the next.

Often guides are asked to retrieve patterns from this source. Once a pattern is located, the Guide must determine whether this particular information will or will not disrupt an experience. Not many linear thought patterns get through this test. There are still more clearings to go through, so the next time you ask a Guide to unscramble a part of your experience by accessing the Akashic, don't be disappointed if you get less than you expect.

It is said that this record is the existence of time encapsulated into all thought that ever was or will be. To measure this essence in a linear fashion would be to date the God Energy Itself, which of course is not possible, for it was in this reality that time became existent.

One article I read said that right after the pyramids were created, Earth went through a catastrophe that wiped out the population.

KIRAEL: Well, the time period is a bit off, but yes, there was a great catastrophe—the Great Flood. The problem is history makes it sound as though it is the story of one man. This is one of the reasons why so many of you are in fear.

In this chapter entitled "Lost Origins," I have tried to point out the simple truth that all present on the Earth plane are going to experience this Shift. The fear that you will experience depends on how veiled you are. This veil can only be reduced if you are willing to move from fear to love and to begin to understand the vast overview.

Please understand one thing: The opportunity to experience the Shift by choice came and went with the time of Master Jesus. This time around, Mother Earth has come into play with a great strength, and She will not be denied. She will no longer tolerate all the destruction placed upon Her.

Your origins are, in fact, not lost. If anything, they are beginning to glow as the time of remembrance starts to permeate all levels of consciousness. All that seems lost is quickly coming to the fore, and those prepared to move with the process will have all the necessary tools.

There will come a time when some future soul will study the great ancient past and will come across this time on some distant planet called Earth that experienced a Great Shift in consciousness. It will be seen that approximately six billion beings entered this Shift, and when all the aspects joined together, two billion energy patterns had been formed.

Now before you do the math, about four billion are destined to leave the planet. Before fear sets in, let us examine the notion of "aspects." Most of you are part of a soul group, and most often, you will have two or three aspects, or incarnations, of Self often right here on Earth. As the Shift hits the apex, the aspects evolving here will merge into one essence (the being of the highest vibration) to process the new understanding.

·8·

Three Days of Darkness

UPDATE FROM KIRAEL

KIRAEL: When I put this one in on the three days of darkness, I had no idea how thrilled everybody was going to be with it. I know they are thrilled. Everybody asks me — me poor medium gets asked this a little bit more than I do because he is on Earth a lot more than I am: When is the three days of darkness going to happen? When is the three days of darkness going to happen?

Well, let me put it to you as best I can. The three days of dark darkness is something that, by the time it happens, you will all be so ready for it, you won't be counting the days. You will be counting the love particles, because, you see, the three days of darkness is when the Earth plane enters into this huge belt of light, and the light is so intensified, there are so many particles that your sun star seems to be blotted out. You say, "Well, God help you, Master Kirael, aren't we going to freeze to death without the sun?" I said, "Seems to be blotted out."

Your Creator makes no mistakes. It knows how to bring enough particles through. Oh, but I am pretty sure that you will be wanting to sleep a lot. In fact, some of you are going to sleep straight through it and not know it happened until it is over.

But here's the good news: As I've already said in the first book, and I will repeat it again, when it is over and you awaken, you are in the throes of the full force of the fourth light and the first thing you will want to do is jump for joy. The second thing you will want to do is get down, because you are going to float up there for quite some time. You see, as you come through that belt, your physical body is readjusted to the light centers. The light centers are the particles that you've carried with you all of your life and waited to ignite in the new state of consciousness.

Now, for all of you out there that we call We the People that just went "WOW," I say this to you as well: Why don't you start now? Why don't you start right now searching through your whole system in every meditation that you have? Search through and say: "I wonder if that is one of those little particles that Master Kirael talked about in his book, *Kirael: The Great Shift?*" And just jostle it a little bit, and if it sparks at you, say "I got one." You might as well, because they are all going to come up one day. But imagine, just imagine, having some right now.

That is what the three days of darkness is truly all about, so stop being a 'fraidy cat. Let yourself know the love of your Creator will not let anything happen to you.

•••

KIRAEL: Let me open this chapter with a deep concern: Whenever any fear slips in, my apologies will be loud and clear, for that is not the purpose of this work. I want to avoid it at all costs. The three days of darkness are not about fear and panic but about ascension into the Fourth Dimension. I extend my apologies over and over again for any fear that might arise, and please understand that I am not trying to scare you. I am trying to prepare you for ascension. The Shift is about love, and any fear you feel is what you have chosen. Choose wisely, my friends, for the Shift will be the start of an awakening to behold.

The three days of darkness actually pertain to Mother Earth's entry into the Photon Belt. This will produce the three days of darkness, and this event heralds the beginning of the Shift, or ascension, into the Fourth Dimension. Let me give you a brief explanation of what will happen during this period. The whole event will take place over a period of seven to ten days or so, but please don't hold me to these numbers because it can fluctuate a day or so either way.

First Day

There will be the sense of complete and utter turmoil at this point. It is not to create fear. Yes, the fear is allowed by the Creator, but you do not have to enter into this fear. Those of you who read this work will be aware of the events that will transpire during this period. You will say to yourself, "This is exactly what Kirael said would happen." You will still have to fight off the fear though, because it will permeate the Earth plane. It is an awakening of a very deep cellular memory that must come to the surface. This is contrived by the light beings to make sure that everybody gets through the Shift by really healing their fears. And, again, because you live so much in fear, you actually do so many good things from fear. Healing your fears is all part of the Creator's design.

This is another reason why you should be attempting to deal with your current fears. As you become practiced in dealing with and dissipating your fears, you will be better able to cope with the Shift. Some fears that you face today are things such as: Are my bills paid?

Will I remain married, and if not, what shall I do? Will I lose all my money on some silly investment? These are, of course, very real, but when looked at in reality, all you need to do is confront the issue and be willing to handle it to the point where the issue comes to total clarity. Then guess what? It always turns out to be not that great big monster you saw. In fact, it becomes extremely manageable for the most part. This is why I emphasize that you complete all your self-learning projects on a timely basis. When you have learned as best as possible to deal with your fears, it will make the Shift an adventure as opposed to a nightmare. Practice makes perfect.

So, in the very first day, you will vibrate with the illusion of mass illness and seemingly devastating disruption. You will literally be leaving the Third Dimension and caught up in the Fourth Dimension, with the Photon Energy mixing in. You will sense the Earth's shifting, major shifting, more so than you may have ever felt up to that point. You will quite literally not want to be walking around in the first 12 hours or so of this first day. You will literally be forced to remain stationary.

This is Mother Earth's way of coming to a screeching halt. In this period, She shakes Herself out and realigns many of Her aspects. All of this is already mapped out, and She knows just how far to go without knocking Herself completely off course. So that will be one of your very first indications: the appearance of massive turmoil followed by Mother Earth really rumbling.

You will have had a number of earthquakes prior to this. Earthquakes will have become almost commonplace by this time. I am not talking about your big eights or nines on the Richter scale but fives, sixes, and below, because that's where Mother Earth will show that She is just getting ready. However, when She gets into Her final Shift position—where the energy of the dimension is going from the Third Dimension to the Fourth and the Photon Energy has already begun to engulf Earth, She will set the stage for Her last spins through the Third Dimension. Therefore, for about 12 to 16 hours on that first day, you will literally have a difficult time staying upright. Don't panic! Do you know how many times you need to be reminded of this? Please don't panic! If you do not panic in these first few hours, things will begin to settle themselves because the rocking and rolling will begin to taper off.

Next, some of the other features that will begin to manifest are the decrease in temperature and sunlight. It will actually begin to look like late evening for the next couple of days. You won't get to see much sun from here on, until you get out of this part of the Shift.

In that time, an awesome awakening will begin to manifest. Depending on your extrasensory abilities, those friends or relatives who have passed onto the other side will be able to communicate with you. This will enable you to work in a way that most have not experienced in this current embodiment. This is just one more reason why, for the past few years, the Guides who know of the Shift have been recommending MEDITATION. My Truth tells me that the word should be upper case, for that is the importance I place on it.

Second Day

Increasing darkness will have begun to permeate the Earth plane, along with a cold never before experienced. It will be a deep cold, for it will penetrate inside of you. At this time, you will make a connection with other entities that are not carbon-based. Here is another reason why you cannot live your life based in fear: You will be faced with what will appear to be some of your greatest tests. All you will need to understand is that IT IS A TEST. You will need only hold onto the Light, for in using the white light, your awareness peaks and the test will disappear.

Third Day

On the third day, Mother Earth will fully enter the Photon Belt and the actual Shift to the Fourth Dimension will occur. This will be where the Photon Energy envelops the Earth plane and the three days of darkness begin. The outer band of the Photon Energy is very dense in order to sweep out the third-dimensional essence and to ignite the fourth-dimensional energy. It will be dark because the light particles are so dense that they take on the appearance of no light. It will take approximately three days to get through this outer band,

and it will appear as if you are in total darkness. Now, do not wake up 72 hours later, walk outside and say, "That's it! I'm out of here." You will have to pay attention and not be hung up on time, for that will become the trickster and cause the energy to take even longer to calm.

As you move into the Photon Energy, it will literally block out the sunlight. This will be the real darkness, my friends. The essence of the Photon Energy literally has the ability to block out the sunlight, so when I talk about darkness, I'm talking about the real purity of darkness. However, some of the sun's thermal energy will get through so you won't have to experience an "Ice Age." It won't be that severe, but trust that it will get extremely cold. Your body will undergo a vibrational shift to compensate for the lack of mobility that most will experience.

It won't make sense to try to go out and fix anything. It won't make sense to try to go down to the corner store to see if it's open. You will not starve to death; nobody will starve to death in three days. In the first place, your metabolism will change so that you won't need food. You will ingest only the lightest of substances. In the beginning, there will be only that which the Creator has brought light to in the form of the plant world. This is what the Creator always supplied you. For whatever reason, you haven't used it wisely up until this point. Now, you will not only utilize plants wisely but you will also learn the true essence of their vibration. I'm sure some will have a bit of a time resonating with this but most will actually begin to enjoy this new food source.

How can people in warm climates prepare for this period? Not by buying ten blankets or building some sort of cold-proof room. The medium reminded me of when he was a young lad and all the people were building shelters in the Earth and stocking them with canned foods. This was in response to someone possibly dropping some sort of giant bomb and the only safe place was in some sort of shelter. Let me assure you, my friends, none of that will be necessary this time. By the time this event actually engulfs your Earth plane, those who are destined to experience the fullness of the event will have learned about vibrational body transfer and motion alliance, so the essence will be completely protected.

Be clear that body energy will get everybody through. That's why it will be important to embrace your brothers and sisters in love. You won't freeze to death because you will have learned about meditation and vibrational body transfer. All these things you are learning on this very mundane level are actually preparation for a time not so far into the future.

In the middle of these three days of complete darkness and cold, most of the world's population will be immobilized. You will slow down to such a state that the three days of darkness won't feel like current time does, my friends. That's how some of the fear will be displaced. You will hardly even remember going through this part of the density. Once it's started and you hit the first of the three days, you'll literally go into a state of hibernation within yourself.

After The Shift

Coming out on the other side of those days of darkness will be beyond your wildest expectations. As the darkness dissipates, you will have another two or three days before it becomes daylight again. It will appear as dusk. When you take your first step, you will realize you no longer touch the ground like you used to. You will find that you can take a hop into the air, stay there a little while, and kind of float back down. There will be pockets of this new energy still somewhat thick so this may be a little tricky at times.

You will feel something new moving through your body and will find that you can fill your body with this new energy that radiates within. From top to bottom, you will love this new feeling that will completely overwhelm the new you.

It will take two to four years for most to learn how to deal with this newness under the guidance of teachers who will carry you through this new reality. They will be honored for what they share, and you will appreciate all those who practiced on this side to learn the art of manifesting. Can you begin to understand why it's so important for all to get the lessons completed before the Shift? That way, there will be no need to experience them afterwards.

As a caution, let me remind you that you will take any unfinished experiences into this new reality, so before the Shift, prepare as much as possible so as not to have to waste precious time while others are moving at the new pace.

You will wonder why you're not hungry because of how much time has passed. Not only will you not have the slightest bit of hunger pain but most, if not all, of your body fat will be gone. When you finally do get hungry, you will recognize that you need to eat something that God created. Then you'll look at the plants that have always been there but that you never really noticed before. You'll pick one of them, put it in your mouth, and it will slowly dissolve. You'll feel its energy emanate into your system. Then suddenly, you'll realize that you are breathing differently. Your breath will come in through the crown of your head and will fill your body in a manner you are not really accustomed to. In those first few days after the Shift, you will learn how to function with everything that is different.

Many new things will occupy your new and enlightened thinking process. Your thought process will be so clear, and your memory will be beyond anything you will have prepared for. You will have approximately 2,000 years to revel in the glory of the Fourth Dimension.

In essence, my friends, although it will seem like a rather shaky situation, this is the beginning of a period of total enlightenment. Most of you have been preparing for many lifetimes just to remember the totality of ascension. Nothing has been wasted, so don't ask, "Why didn't I just wait for this instead of going through all the trauma?" Learn with a great desire so as not to take any old baggage into this new and exciting era.

This is just the beginning. Don't judge the total experience by this short span of time and most certainly, DON'T PANIC!

Questions and Answers

How much linear time do we have left? I mean, we've got to get cranking to raise our vibrations. Can you tell us about when the Shift will take place?

KIRAEL: As I explained before, the actual time frame is irrelevant. It is not the *when*; it is, in fact, *the journey*. So much depends on Mother Earth and Her vibrational system.

As Mother Earth's vibrations increase, this actually slows Her speed towards the null zone. In this time, the masses can more fully prepare for ascension. Ironically, the more you try to prepare from fear, the faster you're going to move towards it. So your challenge, my friends, is to figure out how to teach without fear.

Master Jesus came here to teach without fear. Buddha came here to teach of balance and no fear. All the Masters have tried to teach without fear. However, the human thought process and the lack of 12 DNA strands have allowed some people to use fear to control the masses and gain from a more personal standpoint.

The light cannot be hammered in. It can only be accepted in. If you wish to move this Photon Energy and keep it at bay until you can get more of the population prepared for it, then you must become more enlightened. Don't go into fear. The Photon Energy is coming and you can't stop it. But the more brothers and sisters you are able to prepare for the Shift, the more beauty and light you shall all share in the Fourth Dimension.

I read in a book about the "null zone." Can you tell me about this and how it relates to the Shift and the three days of darkness?

KIRAEL: During the three days of darkness, the Earth's magnetic field will drop to zero and all electromagnetic activity will cease. This is the "null zone," and marks the shift from the Third Dimension into the Fourth Dimension. As we move into the Fourth Dimension, time is already compacting. This is literally compacting the planetary system itself so that the landmasses of Mother Earth are being compressed into a different space. This is going to create shifts for the continents, oceans, and waterways. Thus, it is a physical shift as well as the energy changes that will enable Mother Earth to cleanse Herself.

This sounds like a fearful time, like we're going to have earthquakes. So if I know this now, there would be no fear because I would know what was happening, right?

KIRAEL: Easy to say, but memory is also cellular. It would not be the kind of fear you deal with on an everyday basis. Though many will be aware, for the most part, the masses will be in reaction. We have already talked about the mass consciousness, so you can begin to see the importance of not falling prey to the thoughts of others. Clarity will be at a premium, and those who are fully aware will be able to help others understand. Don't panic. Do you know how many times you need to remember this? Don't panic.

Will the Shift occur the same way all over the Earth?

KIRAEL: The answer is a resounding yes. This is a total Earth Shift. No single place is spared the process. Why would anyone want to miss it? This period of unrest is only a prelude to all the beautiful energy of the Fourth Dimension. The essence of the Earth will be at the highest possible vibration that it has been in for literally thousands of years.

Without electricity and gas, how do we survive? How about cooking food, hot showers, radio, television?

KIRAEL: From our side, one of the most interesting parts of this event is the answers to these particular questions. Most have become so reliant on the creature comforts of this world that they can't begin to understand how they will be able to survive. There are two parts to this: First, as you lose electrical power, Photon Energy will replace it. Remember that your reliance on fossil fuels is one of the things that keeps you hostage to the cartels of this time. The purity of life without all the trappings will soon be the absolute highest form of understanding.

Second, the Galactic Brotherhood will assist you in the conversion of energy. They will move swiftly to see that the most important needs are taken care of. You cannot imagine the speed with which they will assist the remaining essence on this plane.

Can you discuss the other Realms involved in the Shift?

KIRAEL: Mother Earth, like all other entities, is a living, breathing entity, just as your body is a living, breathing entity. Your physical body seems small compared to your totality, but it is alive and well. The duration of the null zone will be uncomfortable for any physical body that is not "lightened up." There are two energies that you can work with entering the null: sound and light, because your third-dimensional body is a molecular structure also composed of light.

Your physical bodies and the human element are among the lower vibrations in the universes. That is not being negative; it is just truth. But that's what you chose when you decided to become part of the DNA reduction. For explanatory purposes, we'll say that with the density you have, you are on the lower end of the spectrum. Different ranges exist on the higher spectrum, such as the Angelic Realm and the Guidance Realm. The Guidance Realm is where I come from. Master Jesus and many of the other Melchizedeks—all of the Great Masters who have manifested into light body—exist in the Guidance Realm. Beyond the Guidance Realm, there exist Light Beings, which permeate every living entity essence in all universes.

Above Light Beings, we have what we call the "Outer Light Band," which is where more concentrated forms of Light Beings exist along with the Akashic Record. Beyond that, we come to the Christ Consciousness, and the totality of the Creator Energy.

Does that mean that I can still buy that car I want, and that house, too?

KIRAEL: This is one of the most important questions in this book. If you remember nothing else, let it be this.

If in reading this book you find yourself saying, "There's no need to buy something or enter into a long term agreement because when the Shift happens, it's not going to have any bearing," then catch yourself. You couldn't be making a more reckless statement. Your life plan calls for certain experiences and each is meant to bring a new level of understanding. Each time you choose to shortcut a lesson, it is simply deferred to the new reality for you to work on then. No matter what, do not deny the possibilities of experience.

Imagine if you would, that you awaken in an energy where all has moved to a space only dreamed about in the past. As you look around and see the potential of life, it is so beautiful that it is breathtaking. You begin to understand about your new body and the capabilities within this new reality. However, due to an incomplete learning situation, your higher self lays out a plan whereby you must repeat an experience. While all your being wants the new energy, it cannot move until all has been mastered. Therefore, leave no possibilities undone. Master everything your higher self lays before you with passion, for this is what brings you into this new millennium.

I know that I have the Light within me, but how do I light it?

KIRAEL: This question can be answered in many ways, yet it will always come back to the three basics of understanding the inner workings of human existence. First and foremost is meditation, followed by automatic writing, and then, what is referred to as sleepstate programming. With these three simple tools, you can work through any and all trials set forth on this journey.

How to light the Light? It is already lit. You only need to know how to bring it to its fullest potential. Use any or all the above to start yourself on that journey.

I didn't know there were different levels of Light Beings. Is Master Jesus the Christ Consciousness?

KIRAEL: Master Jesus Christ and other Masters are, in a sense, in service to the Christ Consciousness. The Christ Energy sits above that Lower Light Band. Above that is the "Upper Light Band," and then the Creator Energy Itself. These different levels do not exist other than in a third-dimensional mind. That's why we break them down to that level. When you have left the Third Dimension after the Shift, the Light Beings will be the ones who will move you into the light-bodied system.

So in a sense, what you are saying is that as we work on the different disciplines we have in the Third Dimension, like the different yogas and different scriptures, these disciplines help our bodies raise our vibration. What we're doing is opening the space within us. If these practices are understood in the deeper sense, we are opening ourselves so the light will fill the vessel. The more we open, the more light we let in. If we do it too quickly, without the right preparation, we can create a space where that light could be very damaging or very overwhelming. So the process is in our journey through the teachings of the Masters, to open slowly, gently, with the full intention of allowing

the light to fill us effectively. So we do this step-by-step and the Shift allows us to move into a space where we can empty out a little quicker than prior years?

KIRAEL: You are absolutely right. I will add a couple of things that may help you to relate further. You're right when you say you cannot blast it full of light because you will dissipate it. The first thing that most want to do when they are filled with so much light is return home to the Creator. That is all right except that it defeats the evolutionary track of the Earth plane. You've gotten 2,000 years behind schedule because the Shift was actually planned for the time of Master Jesus, but the Earth plane was in no way near ready. Most people were not ready to move on, so the outcome would have been catastrophic. Therefore, the evolution process planned by the Creator would have generally failed, and the Creator Essence could not have evolved its own thought patterns into the evolutionary system of which it desired. So in truth, you're absolutely right, but in practice you've got to be careful with it because we don't want to slow anybody down or burst anyone either.

The reason people like you have come into embodiment is to teach, and teachers are those who are willing to change, to put themselves out in front of the crowd, and say, "Here is my best shot. Accept what you like and put the rest away until you're ready."

What you have just stated here is in truth. As the Shift comes about, people need to be ready because the density that you now experience will not align on the other side of the Shift.

How does the Shift relate to the Christ Energy?

KIRAEL: The Master will watch over this whole process with a gleam in His resonance, for this was His true reality from the beginning of time. His is the energy with which all will be again cleansed. When they speak of His second coming, my friends, it is at hand. His energy has really never left the conscious plane of this planet, yet most choose to see this beautiful Light at a distance. Believe that He is not here just when you need Him, for He *is*.

Simply begin to practice the "I Know." The Truth will in fact set you on a path that will enlighten you to the understanding of which Master Jesus spoke: "Whatsoever I do, so shall you."

·9·

Ascension

UPDATE FROM KIRAEL

KIRAEL: In the final chapter of this book, I have talked about something that you've read all the way through the book. This isn't one of the books where you get to the last chapter to know the glory of it. This is one of the works where you utilize every particle of every word, for ascension, me friends, is the awakening of every cell in your body. It is the awakening to know that your thoughts are the manifestations of the All That Is. And then you wake up one day and you say: "My God, it is the particle-zation of manifestation." And you never slow down from that day forward.

Ascension means that you recognize who you are now and you begin the evolutionary ascension to the full flavor of being a human incarnate. You never again look at yourself as "poor me, why would I come to a place like this?" Ascension means that you are already so fully connected, in love, to love, that the oneness within becomes the purity of your guidance. You'll never struggle until you decide it is time to struggle. And even then, after you have read about ascension, you'll know that the part you thought was a struggle is nothing more than an opportunity to fill in a space that the Creator wants to reexperience, and you will look at that and you will be so honored, so thrilled.

So ascension, you want to see what it looks like? Stand up from this book and go look in the mirror. You *are* the ascension of the Creator. You've come here; you've gone through it all, my friends.

Lifetime after lifetime, you've done it all. And you've been chosen; you've been chosen to raise the vibration of a beautiful being called Mother Earth. You've been told to cradle her in your heart. You've been guided to lift her spirit. You've been shown to look up at Father Sky and to watch them merge in a unified force of love that can only be created from the love of Creation itself. And then you will know what ascension is. Ascension is the awakening to the Great Shift in Consciousness.

●●●

KIRAEL: This is not our final chapter, but rather the beginning of the unfolding of the knowingness of ascension. Ascension, in its purest form, is what the Shift is really about. For years, people have talked about the thrill of this process, knowing that someday, hopefully, they would experience it in their lifetime. Well, my friends, the time is a lot closer than you might imagine. After moving along at what seems like a snail's pace for the past few thousand years, the time has finally come to move into the new millennium and to begin to experience the totality of the Fourth Dimension.

In the ascension process, you will have to allow the fears you carry within your cellular memory to be brought to the surface and healed. This will not be the smoothest of transitions in that many will find it overwhelming. Those not ready to move may, of course, want all their friends to stay by trying to convince them that this is just another empty dream. Well, they are not as wrong as you may think. The new space that you will enter into is very much like a dream, only it is anything but empty. The dream that you have been working to understand will finally make sense. You will understand what separates you from the presence of grace. The new knowing is what most have been striving for as long as they have been incarnating on Earth.

The promise that one day you would be able to transcend the gap between your energy and that of the Creator is finally being fulfilled. There *is* no space. It has all been an illusion created to facilitate the journey of experiencing All That Is.

Each has been able to initiate and experience every possible program in existence, only to discover that the plan was drawn up much in advance. The plan, if not fully understood, could be and would be processed in the future, moving into a new incarnation.

Now time has run out. Why are you so fortunate to be part of this latest journey? The only way for an evolving entity to have become a part of this period was to have committed to a life span that included multiple lessons running concurrently before coming into the Third Dimension.

From the first memory, it was evident that upon entering this plane, you had to really step up the pace of your experiences and bring them to completion. That was the only acceptable result, for ascension was the final divine approval.

Let this stand as the start of the journey to Self.

The Fourth Dimension

The Fourth Dimension is the essence of pure thought, and anything and everything that exists in the Third Dimension must have originated in the Fourth. It is, in fact, the bridge between the learning space that humans occupy and all other realities. It is a space that all evolving entities can access. They can communicate and share the learning while still affording the luxury of self-learning. As the Shift gathers momentum and allows humans a new and exciting place to evolve, the Fourth becomes the newest of schoolhouses, but one that will have little or no resemblance to the one you're leaving.

As you enter into the Fourth Dimension, the collapse of the Third Dimension creates a vacuum. This creates a pulling force that automatically draws fifth-dimensional energy towards the current Shift, and you will discover the dimension of love. Your journey into the Fourth will be relatively short. You will learn at a rapid rate, and then all that will be left will be to return to how you once were in Lemuria.

Once you have attained the level of the Fourth, you no longer have the grasp on fear that has permeated the Third. Therefore, advancing to the Fifth Dimension becomes a given. You will remember your existence on the Lemurian plane soon after awakening into the Fourth Dimension. The galactic energy that you may be carrying will be set aside as the love energy you seek becomes the rule. The Fourth offers a multitude of new experiences, and you will want to spend a long time in it.

Portals

Portals are circular energy patterns, and as you go through them, they will cleanse and transport you into the new thought patterns of the Fourth Dimension. Portals will allow you to understand more about your own embodiment, as they are the entrances to the Shift itself. At the portals, portal workers will assist those entering the new dimension.

As soon as you pass through the portal, the cleansing begins. This is where all the unnecessary energies that you may have been carrying are removed. Suppose that you have a cancer or tuberculosis or any kind of illness. For the most part, this will be removed, allowing for a fresh start. Since all your third-dimensional illnesses were created for self-learning within the Third Dimension, you will discover that you don't want to create illness. You will evolve beyond 99 percent of this. Your molecular structure and physical embodiment will come into a much different alignment. Your metabolic rate will change, your heart realigned, and your brainpower expanded. Your embodiment will change—larger kidneys, better blood pressure, and so on.

If you are around 50 years old at the time of the Shift, it is safe to add as much as 130 to 150 years. The average life span can easily reach into the high hundreds. Even this can be extended, if it is desired. You choose.

The portals will actually be fully open prior to the three days of darkness, but they will not be evident at all. After the three days of darkness, they will be extremely evident. By then, the Galactic Brotherhood will already have made their presence known.

Internal portal workers will be those who are already evolved into the Fourth Dimension and they will help others to evolve in a gentler, loving fashion. They will also help to dispel any residual fear.

External portal workers will experience the Shift from the highest element. It's difficult to explain in third-dimensional terms; however, if you have chosen to be an external portal worker, know that you made the commitment before coming onto the Earth plane. The commitment probably saved you 10 to 12 lifetimes in the Fourth or Fifth Dimensions, and you will be rewarded in the light of Master Jesus and all of the Grand Masters who will be there in assistance. All of you will be light beings, and once in the portal, you will feel the love of the Fifth Dimension.

The Galactic Brotherhood

After the three days of darkness, the Galactic Brotherhood will be quite protective. Remember, they have been in and out of your dimension much longer than your recorded history. Immediately after the three days of darkness, you will awaken and find yourself surrounded by chaotic situations. To help everyone to remain calm, the Galactic Brotherhood will assist in creating a safe atmosphere. They will be your guides, helping you to understand the new power that you will be experiencing.

You will need time to adjust to your new and expanded roles, and this is where your brethren will be of the most service. Remember that most evolving souls have remnants of the galactic within them and you will resonate to their vibration. In a sense, they will be welcoming you home. You see, after the Atlantis melding, it became apparent that the Brotherhood was in the position to begin their understanding of a larger heart role. So when they do have an opportunity to help, they will want to do all that is possible.

Post-Shift Changes

As we move into the new dimension, everything changes, my friends. Everything changes! You will not recognize the Earth plane as you recognize it today. Your body systems will change. You will awaken talents and techniques that are currently mind-boggling to you. For instance, if you wanted to see a long distance friend, you would simply think, "I want to be there." You would disappear and reappear there. This ability may seem foreign to most and stretch your thinking process, but if you had told your grandfather when he was a child that in his lifetime there would be a vehicle on Mars sending pictures back in 44 seconds, surely he would have scoffed. So there are many beautiful things about the Shift that will transpire, but you must first get there.

The rebirth of your powers will astound you because your body will experience many physical changes post-Shift. The cranium will expand to allow for new brain activity. Some of you have already experienced this. In order to activate the remaining parts of your brain on a fourth-dimensional level, you will need more space in there. Possibly your head could begin to look like those of your ET brothers who you thought looked a bit funny. You won't be laughing quite so hard after the Shift when you look back at the pictures of what you looked like before. Your great-grandchildren will look at pictures of you as you are today, and say, "Ho! Look at that! Were they weird or what?"

The eyes, too, will go through an extreme set of wonderful changes. Your vision will be what it was long, long ago when you were able to look directly into a molecular structure. Now understand that the molecular structures will be different in the Fourth Dimension. However, there will be a certain way of breaking down the structure and being able to re-focus without breaking down the next particle.

Your breathing will change as you ascend, with prana breathing becoming the energy source that the body functions best with. Remember that prana was what you existed on during your lifetimes in Lemuria, when the only thing you used your breath for was to oxygenate the system. Your energy pattern was sustained by prana. In the Fourth Dimension, prana from the Photon Energy will be your main source of life. So practice prana breathing now, for it will revitalize and replenish your cells and cleanse your cellular consciousness. That is one of the many reasons why your life span will increase dramatically.

Control of the size of your body will be just a matter of thought controlled by desire. Skinny or heavy will be simply a choice. Post-Shift, this will not matter. All you will care about is that your body be suitable for the particular journey being undertaken.

You will also have less skin pigmentation, and that will be very shocking for some. Your vocal chords will also diminish considerably because you will use them primarily for humming, Om-ing, and singing. The rest of your communication will be done telepathically.

Now, there is no magic to telepathy. You each have this ability right now. In fact, most of you are already using it consistently, but you dismiss it by saying one of two things. If you read another's thought while they are transmitting, you may say, "Wow, that was really weird!" Well, it's not weird. That is the way you are supposed to communicate! Or you may say, "No, that didn't happen. I just made a lucky guess." Okay, let's question this luck. How many times a day do you think you can create that luck?

Let's suppose that there are 50 people in this room, and 25 of you know how to use your telepathic powers. How would that influence your thoughts as you think them? Would that not clean your thinking up just a bit? How about if one-eighth of the world was telepathic? There are in Africa, for instance, a number of tribes who hardly speak; they communicate almost totally telepathically.

Your mental telepathy and intuitive understanding will be enhanced by the clarity that resonates within you. As most of your communication will be done by thought, it would only make sense to be very clear. This is not the case now. In fact, it seems most are intentionally trying to make others think they are something other than what they truly are. You figure that one out!

In the ascension process, your memory will be enhanced to levels never conceived of before. You are going to remember everything that has ever happened to you in all of your lifetimes combined. You will have a complete memory of a lifetime back in Egypt or China, and you will say, "Oh, so that's why I've been living like this." You will be able to answer all the little questions that you've been carrying around with you all these years and will understand exactly what's happening with you. You are going to change, my friends, for these are just some of the many new and exciting possibilities that you will experience.

After the Shift, the one thing that most people will be mindful of is the awareness of their emotions. When you are finally in the Fourth Dimension, your emotions will be something that you will use as entertainment. You will have such a grand understanding of your emotions that you will be able to activate any feeling at will. Your emotional experience will be different in that you will not have the uncontrolled peaks and valleys that you now experience. As a post-Shift light being, you will have freed yourself from many, if not all, of the suppressed emotions of the Third Dimension. Remember, your base chakra will become the green, heart center. This means that you will experience from the heart rather than from the ego, which is so absolutely beautiful! Your emotions will be expressed from the essence of unconditional love emitted from the Fifth Dimension.

Sex will transcend the physical. What will emerge is the "art of making love." During post-Shift, making love will be an art form of enjoying the entire movement, body rhythms, pulsations and changing colorations, which will determine the level of ecstasy and reveal patterns to explore on even higher plateaus. There will be times during lovemaking that physical contact will be unnecessary, yet the feelings experienced will be unlike anything that you have surrendered to in this space and time.

Be reassured, my friends, you haven't even begun to experience the sensual capabilities of your physical bodies. While immersed in the spiritual essence of love, you will be able to reach heavenly bliss in ways never perceived in this current reality. Now, I suppose, some of you can't wait.

The climate will also change radically. You will have your four seasons, and you could actually enjoy all four seasons in a couple of days because you will control the climate from within yourself. You will control everything from within. If it's cold on the outside and you don't want to be cold, you will just raise your vibration and you will not experience the cold. Conversely, you will be able to lower your vibration and cool off. Thus, it will not be a climate as you recognize today.

To experience this new reality, more and more emphasis will be placed on the openness and freedom to move from place to place. Many will simply sit and be in awe of the beautiful sunsets and the gracefulness of Earth's oceans or mountainous beauty.

It is all about enjoying your life, therefore everything else becomes passé. To enjoy your life is to be in the now. Being in the now will show you all the gifts and blessings that the universe has for you. When someone gives you a hug, enjoy the hug!

Everything is a matter of choice but without the dead weight of duality. Everything is thought. Whatever you think will be created in the now. When you attain the higher levels of this ascension process, most travel will be done ethereally, except when you want the experience of something else and then anything goes.

One of the many thrilling aspects of this newness is the ability to share the inner feelings of love. All will gain a clearer understanding of the different levels of love, with the increased abilities of perception. You will move to the conscious level of discovering your gifts and talents given to you by our Creator. Your essence will be to serve the Earth plane, and you will discover how to maintain the smooth and beautiful transition of growth while still allowing others the space to evolve at their own pace. Please be clear that all are still evolving. The Fifth Dimension will still be the goal of discovery. Lessons will be in abundance as the ascension continues to the Fifth, for there are still many self-learning projects to be completed.

Your job, as you will see, will become a labor of love. It will involve moving away from having an authority figure that uses fear to finish tasks to the perspective that all share a responsibility in seeing the project to completion—not just done, but done to the highest standards so that all involved will know completion. In this, a project will allow for new group resonance, and collectively, a doorway of opportunity to prepare them to enter into the Fifth Dimension. Those who remember the beauty of Lemuria will be reawakened to the councils that once existed. There is much more to do in the Fourth Dimension than you can possibly imagine. You will have 2,000 years to evolve through the Fourth Dimension, so prepare to enjoy it. It has taken many thousands of years to get through the Third Dimension, so it is hoped that at least you have acquired patience.

You will have a multitude of information to process compared to that in the Third Dimension. It has taken you thousands and thousands of years to reach this point, so take the time to recognize the past so as not to repeat the learned lessons. Keep in mind that everyone who makes the Shift will be somewhat of a teacher. You will ask your brothers and sisters for help with the lessons that you have not learned here in the Third Dimension. I love it! Everyone acting in the capacity of teacher in the Fourth Dimension. Imagine a couple of billion teachers running around wondering where all the students are.

Currently in this dimension, you have brainpower and computers but little understanding of non-physical realities. After the Shift, you will move into knowing, and technology will take a major turn. In the beginning, your technology will run on Photon Energy, but you will want to learn to move beyond that. You will want to move towards "demolecularizing." Remember that this is just a stepping-stone to where you are returning—the Fifth Dimension.

Growth there will not be like growth here, that is, from birth to whatever time you choose to leave and go home. What you have called "a life" is the growth track that you chose, with all its experiences. After the Shift, the ability to choose different experiences will be by thought process alone. Imagine if each thought was capable of resonating with all others. What a great way to experience the totality, which is a dimension where love permeates all existence, and where the possibilities become endless.

The Fourth Dimension is about the bliss of learning, so death or moving on will be a time of celebration and asking if there is anything that could be done to further the experience. If not, then the last action will be to bid your loved ones a warm farewell. You won't have funerals or boxes with satin pillows decomposing in the ground. Most will simply choose to dematerialize. By simply holding hands, your energies will join together and whoever is ready to leave, will leave. The joy is beyond your wildest expectations.

Throughout history, you have been embraced within the essence of the God Creator, and now is the most powerful and illuminating time to begin the journey of remembering love. Ascension is the absolute vibration of the All That Is, and as the mass consciousness begins in earnest, the mission will become a collective thrust, making way for each to remember the truth of being "all of the whole" once again.

Questions and Answers

What does "going home" mean?

KIRAEL: When you have undergone all the experiences possible on this journey, you will usually go through a pre-planned process beginning with death. Often this is a major role in the whole plan because for the most part this existence has been permeated by fear. The drama of death will clear and release the cellular fear, so "going home" simply means the return to the Source, or freedom from fear.

In order to prepare for the Shift, does the DNA structure have to be four-stranded or six-stranded?

KIRAEL: Your wording may be a bit off in that, at the printing of this work, most will be experiencing some growth in their DNA. Most will not perceive this until after the actual Shift takes place. A minimum of six strands will be needed to operate at peak efficiency in the Fourth Dimension. In order to allow the strands to vibrate into existence, you will have to conquer fear. One of the purposes of the Third Dimension is to understand cellular fear, and as this becomes clear, the ascension of the DNA will begin its own evolution. Remember that this encoding called DNA is the one aspect each of you brings throughout all of your incarnations.

Is the family structure going to change?

KIRAEL: Change may be an understatement. As the individual members of a family ascend into this new energy, all will have the veils dropped. With this, the games being played in the present will be brought to their completion.

Currently each member of a family has a role. For example, the father is the so-called "breadwinner" while the youngest child may be non-productive and needing the most protection and guidance. In the ascension process, all rules cease. The newest member of a family may be the one, for instance, who will have the guidance to assist the family in moving collectively.

As most ascending beings are considered to be balanced in the male/female essence, the family will be responsible collectively to inspire unity in each member. Members will not be left to evolve on their own. If one should fall behind on experience, all other members will rally to enjoin their energies, raising all to a compatible level.

Your soul family (not to be confused with your third-dimensional family) will become much more apparent to you at that point. It will not be uncommon to realize that your baby sister is your mother from another life. This may be confusing initially, but all will become clear with the reasons laid before you.

How will marriage change?

KIRAEL: There will be no papers, and the ceremonies and all the relationship issues will be based in the Trinity of Truth, Trust and Passion. No other laws will govern this union. You will stay together as long as together equates to growth. If this should end, no official ending process will be needed, for the growth will carry on in a different reality. Entities choosing to share journeys will be considered in relationships, and in that, they will be blessed on the spiritual level and seen to be in loving grace.

What happens to the parent-child relationship?

KIRAEL: Even now, it is becoming more evident that children have a larger contribution than previously believed. I remind parents not to underestimate the ability of these little people. Treat them as guiding souls and their responses will amaze all. Without exception, each newborn has a special understanding of the Shift and how it will relate to the new energy. Be careful not to discourage their growth, and if nothing else, *LISTEN*.

When the child is born, will the parents still have a nurturing and caring role?

KIRAEL: As this new reality is still a journey of remembrance of love, the child will play a major role in completely revamping the old school of raising the young. They will not respond to the fear-based teachings of the past. Therefore, the adult will have to use powers that have lain dormant for a long period of time. This lesson of nurturing will be a test of growth for the parents as well as for the child. If you learn to communicate with love now, the experience will move quite smoothly.

Some of the old possibilities that have been carried along will appear the same, yet the vibration will have ascended. For example, you may say, "Okay, since I missed the birth experience in the Third Dimension, I'd like to know what it's like to come through the birth channel." The chosen mother may then say, "Of course. I, too, missed that over there in the Third Dimension, so let's go ahead and try it out."

Birthing in the Fourth Dimension will be painless. You will get to choose whatever you want to experience. The difference between birthing now and birthing post-Shift is the clarity of knowing the soul that you agreed to bring into the dimension, along with its life experience plan. However, you will not know the outcome of that plan. Still, there will be love and sharing. So remember, love will always be the answer.

Can you explain what "Shift babies" mean?

KIRAEL: The Shift baby began to incarnate around the time of the Harmonic Convergence and has permeated the Earth plane. Each one coming through brings the essence of Mother Earth a special gift. Along with this, if you are fortunate enough to have been a parent in this time, be assured that you are caring for a special part of the new millennium.

The Shift babies can be looked at as adjusters because of the awesome knowledge they have brought which is able to align with the Fourth Dimension, even prior to the Shift. The closer to the Shift they choose to arrive, the more intricate the information these babies bring. Be aware that they need special handling. They will often seem more adult than their parents, and that's because they are.

What will your position be in educating people after the Shift?

KIRAEL: I will have no particular position, as my commitment to establish the reality of the Great Master prior to this process will have been completed. I, of course, will watch those who have interacted with my essence, and because I will hold a special place in my essence for them, I will always be available for guidance. As I will no longer need a medium to converse with the new reality, I shall interact in a greater capacity.

How will the role of the schoolteacher and educator change?

KIRAEL: Drastically. Let's look at what's happening now. For the most part, teachers today are doing more in child management than the parents are. This will change in that the roles will have a significantly different expression. The educator will actually get to teach. The ones who come to the teachers will really want to move forward as compared to now, where they are forced to move at the pace of those who went before them.

Teaching will be something like this. You will ask the Masters for information, such as Master Jesus, and you will get a group of people together to share this information. Then you will return to the Masters for new information. A beautiful example of teaching will be getting some people to place their hands on a tree to communicate with it, for it is God's creation just like you. Trees have been here for many, many years and they are full of wisdom. It will only take the understanding of how to listen to them. If you are currently a teacher, imagine what it will be like to receive information directly from the Masters, which you will then share with others.

Will education be about experiencing the oneness?

KIRAEL: It will be about returning to being your God Self. Beautiful! Only those who are in the state of giving will truly want this type of experience. Truth can be interpreted as evolving into the clarity of oneness.

How will our government and society change?

KIRAEL: The government structure will change radically in that it will revert to the understanding that love is the reality, not fear. There will be no rule, for it's not about ruling. It will be about living in spirituality.

The Hawaiians, the Native Americans, and the other races were ruled by their heart for the most part. Their only rule was understanding your heart. The leaders came in the role of healer and giver, never taking anything for granted. The art of supplying food was where they demonstrated this best. Never was anything taken without permission, for that was how they saw all of evolution reaching together for this golden space.

Will healers be performing the four-body healing?

KIRAEL: Post-Shift healing will actually take on a different reality. Though there will still be a need for aligning the four bodies, the art itself will change. Be clear that the healers in the Third Dimension will always be revered, for when the actual Shift takes place, these healers will be the ones to keep the flow of energy open so that you will be able to adjust with the least amount of separation possible. During post-Shift, their essence will move to even greater levels and most of their love will be spent on the alignment of lateral forces.

In the healing of the emotional body, is the love energy that is coming forth allowing people to gain insight into their experience so they can heal that part of the emotion that is in fear?

KIRAEL: Yes! The reason why we have you working so much on the emotional body is because when you arrive in the Fourth Dimension, the emotion will be one of the things that you will love to play with. That is why we are working so hard to get you all up to snuff! Beautiful!

What about the leaders that will be emerging?

KIRAEL: Again, there will be no leaders. However, you will listen to your channels without seeing them as higher than you. You will accept that those who channel through you have chosen a particular way of assisting. All records will be kept in the ethers, so those who channel will be the gatherers of all that is taking place. Therefore they will have a role but not in a hierarchy. From the third-dimensional perspective, it would appear that they have ascended into a higher state, but they haven't. In the Fourth Dimension, there is no separation. Those of you asked to design levels of teachings will form councils, whose most important goal is to allow another council to replace it.

Will there be a division of countries?

KIRAEL: There will be no real or imaginary boundaries. All essences that have moved to evolution will be seen as one in service to the All That Is. Those who choose otherwise will be honored, for that will be seen as lessons for the All.

Will the law become love?

KIRAEL: Law is something enacted to ensure that unwilling forces are penalized for their inability to choose growth. As no one would make such a choice, there will be no great need for law. Love will prevail, and whenever a question of right or extra right becomes apparent, the entity who exercises the most brilliant form of love and light will help the other find the answer to fit the All.

Epilogue

A Final Thought by the Author

So there you have it. An ever unfolding of the many possibilities! Will this work be subject to scrutiny? I truly pray it will be so. Will others come along and bring even greater clarity to these changing times? I surely can't conceive of it in any other way.

When the majority of this information was released some eight years ago, for the most part it was seen as a "maybe" or, as some would say, "I guess it could happen." The skeptics cast a blanket of doubt—mostly, I guess, in hopes that it was just some irrational behavioral patterns of the unseen forces of light.

Yet, from that day forward, I have forever been answering the question, "When will it happen?" "Give us a date, Kahu, so we can crawl under a blanket and hide from the force." Most were referring to the three days of darkness, and yet, in my humble opinion, when that particular phenomenon happens, it will be but a mere blink of reality. The true Shift has already started, although few have been even aware of the oncoming expression of change.

As close as I can calculate, this expected day is to come to pass exactly in the manner that I have come to accept as a time reference. Kirael has made it abundantly clear that this most awesome Shift in Consciousness will happen when humankind fully embraces their knowing that they actually can control their corner of the universe by submitting the full force of thought into their daily existence. In simple terms, it is when "We the People" stop believing that we are doomed to be controlled by the few and begin to take full responsibility for the unfolding of our life. This is a state of conscious thought that was fully embraced in times such as ancient Lemuria.

The Great Shift in Me

This work, as I like to call it, is still in progress and has literally changed the way I view the entirety of life. In fact, it has helped me to be fully aware that, even as the book was being written, the steady shifting of world vision was already in motion. I began to see life as an unfolding scripted adventure that would not end. I discovered, as

I was writing this work, that I could prepare for the inevitable by simply living my life based upon the principle that everything is subject to my thoughts and that, as long as these brain transmissions were evolving, I would be ever ready for whatever happened.

Oh, yes, my friends, I could find fear if I looked for it. Chaos seemed to be prevalent in everything, and if I dropped my guard for an instant, it simply surrounded me. In fact, the deeper I began to search the pages I had helped to write, the more I came to the clarity that everything I was thinking could manifest and likely would. In that light, what choice did I have? I had to begin living my life as though I was important to the grand plan. I began to see that I was in control, and the more I embraced this idea, the more my life began to expand.

Still, I pondered: Could life be as simple as me deciding what I was going to think? Such a concept seemed so unnatural in comparison with what history had displayed. It was unbelievable to think that I should just sit around and wait for some catastrophic foreboding to engulf the world.

Was I to wait and see how the rest of the spiritual community was going to react? Or was this waiting simply so phenomenal that nothing I did would make any difference anyway. My answer was an emphatic "no," and that, my friends, was what sent me striking out on this whole new way of taking charge of my life. You see, if you erase more and more negative thoughts, they are replaced with the opposite. In that new light, you fill your minds with what you want as opposed to what others want for you. And that, my friend, was my earliest exposure to this ever-shifting energy.

Doom and gloom, chaos and eternal damnation, were stricken from my vocabulary. What replaced them was the wonderment of greatness, ceaseless peace and a whole new drive to understand this journey called life. I became so passionate about the new dimensional vibration I had discovered that nothing else mattered. I became so mesmerized by the potentials being exhibited that I found myself preparing, not for the Great Shift in Consciousness for the Earth plane, but for the immediate transformation I could feel. It started deep within the inner part of my destiny-charged particles of light and began to conjure mystical types of manifestation that in the past I only had the courage to dream about. Now, it seemed, was my chance to pull out all the stops and progress as though the world as I knew it was about to transform into something I could begin to control. What a heavenly thought.

They say that when you begin to realize that you are the creator of your existence, calm seems to take residence in your very soul. They were right. I began to understand that my life was as important as any other and, in fact, I must admit that the thought crossed my mind that it just might be a bit more important. You see, without your own life, nothing really matters anyway, does it? In my heart I knew that if I was going to be part of this Great Shift, I would need to be so fully prepared that I would not miss a single thing. I would want to be at the head of the class, and from that vantage point, I could get the very best experience. What the heck, even with the remote possibility that all this was just a chancy reality, I would still be better off.

In that light I began to truly look for ways to prepare for the Shift. I began to study other world possibilities. In my search for these things, I discovered a world I never knew existed. Here on this planet we could have a life exactly as we could perceive it. There was so much unlearned reality that I didn't need flying saucers or mystical creatures to ignite my already passionate mind. What I did need was the willingness to open my senses to the unfolding world around me, for in this I felt alive once more.

Oh my God, I was shifting already.

So, for many years now, I have watched, not as a spectator but more as a participant, as the world quietly moves from one level of consciously thinking to another. It never stops. The minute I reach a certain plateau, I find it to be the step to another awakening. Never ending in the awareness of thought do I find life worth living!

In his essay *The Myth of Sisyphus,* Albert Camus begins by stating, "There is only one truly philosophical problem and that is suicide." Camus told of a man, Sisyphus, who, having angered the gods, was destined to spend eternity pushing a huge bolder up a hill, and just before he reached the top, it would fall down and he would start over. Though his life never changed, he thought his lot in life better than the thought of death; hence, Camus' essay took on the constant question of whether life is worth living.

Camus went on to say, "Whether the world has three dimensions or the mind nine or twelve categories," nothing truly makes any difference unless We the People are convinced that life is worth living. In truth, that is life in a nutshell. As long as we are challenged by evolution and accept such a challenge, we will continue to fill in the details in making this life worth living.

The Great Shift in You

This work is meant to challenge the thinker. It is written by a Master Guide whose energy exists in a totally different dimensional pattern of life. It may help to remember that you have just read something that is written on seven different levels of understanding. Almost everyone will perceive it on an individual level first, and in this, the possibility of debate is constant. For this I am ever thankful.

As a reader of this work, you may have experienced elation, anger, fear or an even more desirable feeling—that all this so-called reality somehow begins to make sense. Whatever you have felt, just keep remembering that we are already speeding towards this entirely new way of understanding. From the time of Aristotle, through Newton, and even in the work of Einstein, it has come to be expected that each new way of viewing the universe is subject to change.

One such theory that the world of science is working on is the connection of something called the string theory. In lay terms, scientists are attempting to prove the existence of something within the light particles that actually connect the huge or infinite, such as stars, with the infinitely miniscule, including particles within the human body and everything else in between.

The difference is that we now have beings of Light from alternate dimensions sharing "deep thought information" with us. We have been a little slow on the uptake of accepting it, yet we are slowly but surely gaining the strength to question the so-called realities that have perpetuated our evolution. Over the years, it has never ceased to amaze both me and an ever growing number of Lightworkers that what Kirael spoke of years ago is somehow magically being introduced to the masses as a brand-new discovery by the scientific community.

From my heart, I thank you for opening your soul to the infinite possibilities that this work offers. I know it is not really my business, yet I recommend that you not give this work to a friend. I strongly feel it is better to set it on the shelf and wait for the inevitable calling to pick it up again. Such has been my experience in talking to those who have read it, and given it away, and are still trying to get their copy back.

Over the years I have had people show up at book signings literally with a copy of the original *Kirael: The Great Shift* in pieces. I have asked them if I could replace their copy with a new one and have been rejected. They seem to feel the connection the book offers them about choice.

There have been stories of mothers putting the book under their children's pillows, causing them to sleep better. Another woman once pulled me to the side and whispered that she had experienced severe chest pains and held her copy of the book to her chest until the medical team arrived. She shared that she felt it was the confidence that the work had shown her that caused her to be calm enough to live on.

Why do I share this with you? Because these are just a couple of the many shares I have received, and to tell you the truth, I believe them. I firmly trust in the knowing that "thought" can and will change the flow of existence.

In my journey I know that, at some point in time, we will all, in one manner or another, be talking to the unseen forces of Light, or guides, as some wish to call them. It just so happens that, in my journey, it is happening in the now. Enjoy, marvel, question and forever more prepare for the most powerful and uplifting adventure we as humans have ever had the opportunity to experience, as we move from one level of consciousness to another.

Just maybe, this is "The Great Shift."

My friends, I pray that you are enjoying your Great Shift as much as I am enjoying mine.

Kahu Fred Sterling
March 25, 2005
Honolulu, Hawaii

About Fred Sterling

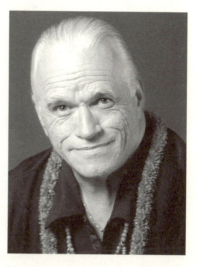

Fred Sterling is a master medium, a minister and a messenger—a shaman of Native American ancestry who walks between the third dimensional world of human and the boundless realms of spirit. For more than 15 years, he has channeled the loving light and wisdom of Kirael, a master spirit guide, into books, articles and recorded sessions. As founder and Senior Minister of the Honolulu Church of Light, a non-traditional spiritualist church, he shines his own love and light upon both a local congregation and an international community of lightworkers via the Internet.

He has authored several books with Master Kirael, including *Kirael: The Great Shift*; *Kirael: The Genesis Matrix*; *Guide to the Unseen Self*; and *Kirael: The Ten Principles of Consciously Creating,* and shares his wisdom and Kirael's message through frequent radio, Internet and television programs. His weekly, live Internet webcast, "The Great Shift with Fred Sterling," brings many of the top spiritualists and healers from around the world to lovingly awaken us to the great shift in consciousness. Rev. Sterling is, first and foremost, a gifted and dedicated healer, helping seekers around the world discover their own paths of healing into Love.

As a child, Reverend Sterling endured an upbringing of incredible hardship, including life in an orphanage and a succession of six stepfathers. In his earlier years, he held a number of challenging jobs, such as serving as an orderly in a prison for the criminally insane. He survived the most abject poverty imaginable to achieve the life of a successful, affluent businessman—only to give that all up to follow his spiritual calling.

At the Honolulu Church of Light, he has emerged as a pioneering healer and a trance medium of growing distinction. His relationship with the wise and loving Kirael has touched the lives of untold thousands across the globe through his books, tapes, videos and public and private sessions. With the guidance of Master Kirael, he has introduced Signature Cell Healing into the world and created a unique form of long-distance healing that taps the power of a global listening audience. "I'm only 57," he says "but I probably should be 190 for all the experience I've packed into this lifetime."

Fred Sterling has embraced the adventure of life more passionately than most, and what validates his work as minister and healer is precisely this life experience. It has allowed him to cultivate a sense of complete honesty and authenticity—what you see is what you get—and his style on the air or on the street is fully engaged and extemporaneous. All of Rev. Sterling's Sunday Service messages at the Honolulu Church of Light are relentlessly drawn from personal experience; he shares lessons from his own journey, teaching rather than preaching. "I'm a man that needs explanations," he says. "I think that's what makes me a good minister. I have to see everything myself. I can't talk to an audience about something that doesn't make sense in my own life."

Throughout it all, Rev. Sterling downplays his role as "leader" or "healer" and instead, relishes his role as "messenger," wherein the message is more important than the messenger. And while his eyes occasionally flash with the focus and brilliance of the affluent businessman he once was, his demeanor is one of kindness and humility, with a genuine love for people of all spiritual paths.

"My whole journey in life at this point," says Rev. Sterling, "is to let people see that options are available, to not get caught up in the fear or fall prey to the "doom and gloom." I want people to find the beauty and the light within themselves and begin to use it, begin to heal."

About Master Guide Kirael

Kirael is a loving spirit guide from the seventh light that has committed his light into the Earth plane to help humanity heal, evolve and experience what he calls "the Great Shift in Consciousness." Brought forth through the mediumship of Rev. Fred Sterling, Master Guide Kirael has been called King of Angels and Guardian of the Journey.

In recent history, great energies have permeated the Earth plane, bringing information from sources not readily available to the human world. In the 1970"s Jane Roberts brought forth the remarkable non-physical entity called *Seth*. Today, there are many profound and loving energies being channeled to help Mother Earth and her inhabitants:

Kryon, brought forth by Lee Carroll
The Group, through Steve Rother
Abraham, through Esther Hicks
Gaia, through Pepper Lewis
Archangel Michael, through Ronna Herman
and many, many more.

In the late 1980's an exciting new energy force made its presence known to another generation of Lightworkers. It called itself Kirael (pronounced Ki-ra-el), and Rev. Fred Sterling has been honored to act as his medium. We call this entity "he" only because he communicates through Rev. Sterling, yet Kirael has made it clear that his energy pattern is neither a "he" nor a "she" but rather an energy pattern of light from an alternate dimension.

Kirael is here on an unprecedented mission of monumental consequence. He has appeared in this moment of history to fulfill an ancient prophecy—echoed many times throughout the ages—about an evolutionary cycle that began some 200,000 years ago. It is no coincidence that so many great energies are here at the same time, for this is a moment of extraordinary change and growth.

Council Master Kirael, as he is formally known, has come to usher Mother Earth and her inhabitants into a new era of profound evolutionary change, which he has dubbed "the Great Shift in consciousness." This period in history, prophesied through ancient Mayan, Native American, Egyptian and Biblical calendars as well as through Nostradamus and many modern psychics, has been called "The End Times," "Zero Point," "The Time of No Time" and other fearful sounding names. It has elicited vivid images of Armageddon or Ascension, Rapture or Apocalypse.

However, Kirael has consistently maintained that the Great Shift is not about doom and gloom; it is a time of great joy and celebration as Mother Earth rebalances herself and prepares for mass evolutionary movement into a new dimension.

Master Guide Kirael's greatest imperative is the healing of the human world. He has made world peace, harmony and the enlightenment of humanity his major agenda. He has provided powerful, practical tools for the Shift through books and recordings, radio, TV and Internet broadcasts, and a rich website full of article and audio archives.

Great Shift Workshops
&
Signature Cell Healing™
Workshops

To attend a Great Shift Workshop
or a Signature Cell Healing™ Workshop
in your area:

Call toll free, U.S. only:
(800)-390-1886
or
visit our website:
www.Kirael.com

Principles of Consciously Creating

Since the original publishing of *Kirael: The Great Shift*, Master Guide Kirael has provided much information regarding what he calls the Ten Principles of Consciously Creating.

The Ten Principles of Consciously Creating are powerful tools of awakening that, when studied and practiced, allow you to create the life you truly desire. In short, they are "keys for awakening," with each Principle a key to unlocking higher levels of conscious awareness and tapping into your own powers of creation.

The Ten Principles are all magically interwoven; however, the most basic grouping is:

- Truth, Trust and Passion (the Trinity or the Three Keys), which anchor the Love of the Creator within the Self.

- Clarity, Communication and Completion (the Three Commitments), which guide our thoughts and actions in our daily lives.

- Prayer, Meditation, Sleepstate Programming and Masterminding (the Four Pillars), which are the practices that help you to manifest your dreams and heartfelt desires.

A more in-depth look at all ten principles is offered in the book, *Kirael: The Ten Principles of Consciously Creating*, or in CD or audio tape versions, titled *How to Have It All: The Ten Principles of Conscious Creation,* available at www.kirael.com. However, short descriptions of Sleepstate Programming and Masterminding are included here since they are discussed in *Kirael: The Great Shift.*

Sleepstate Programming

Sleepstate Programming is Principle 9 of *The Ten Principles of Consciously Creating*.

What is sleepstate programming?

Sleepstate programming is the practice of enlisting your own higher self to contact and communicate with the higher self of another during sleep.

The average human spends between six and eight hours in the sleep state. The common thought is that sleep is virtually a waste of time. However, the essence of your consciousness is pure energy and is in constant motion. In truth, your higher self has total freedom to move to whatever space it desires. This may include dimensional travel, switching realities, journeying to outer solar systems, or simply having fun in the world of dreams. Your higher self can be left to randomly move into whatever space it chooses or it can enlist the Guidance Realm to take action. Interestingly, as you move into the higher vibration of consciousness, your ability to recall these travels is expanded dramatically.

The higher self is not limited by the physical realities of the third-dimensional body. Therefore, it has no boundaries and can be programmed to perform certain functions that the physical body cannot. Remember, this whole adventure called "life experience" has been laid out with growth as the master plan. Anything with a potential for growth can be worked on in the highest order.

The simplicity of sleepstate programming is probably its largest deterrent, as many believe that in order for anything to be of real value, it must be either extremely complicated or very expensive.

Here is masterminding in its simplest form. Just before going to sleep, ideally after meditating, take a few deep inhalations to relax the mind and body, and begin a dialog with your higher self. It may sound something like this: *"I know you have had the freedom to do whatever you desired in the past. This evening I request that my directions be followed to the letter, prior to the usual journeys of intention."*

This will get you on the right heading. Remember, this is going to be quite new and will look as though you are stifling the higher self, so be gentle. Now if a situation in your life involves another person, the conversation may continue like this: *"I've been working on a situation for some time with little success. As I have not been able to reach a mutually agreeable outcome with this person, I would like you to meet with the higher self of this other person and work out the following details in the following manner."* Details are essential at this point because your higher self is perfectly capable of producing the results in the exact manner you prescribe.

The conversation may end in this manner: *"Oh, yes, by the way, I also want to have a clearer memory of my dreams, so please keep the reality of my dreams in the upper essence of my mind until after I wake so that I may write them down."* You may get as involved as you desire knowing that the clearer and more impassioned your communication with your higher self, the better the result.

You can use this simple technique to make fuller use of a time you previously thought was wasted. The results can be overwhelmingly successful, so be prepared to be pleasantly surprised. Once you are comfortable with the technique, you can use it in all areas of your life—the possibilities are endless. However, many of the more rewarding aspects of this technique require practice of the Ten Principles of Consciously Creating to develop it to its apex.

Lastly, it must remain clear that the most important component of this miraculous journey you are venturing into depends upon the level of passion you bring forth. Let your reality burst into the light, and begin to experience the success of working with your higher self.

Masterminding

Masterminding is Principle 10 of *The Ten Principles of Consciously Creating*.

What is a mastermind?

A mastermind is a thought form or mental construct held by more than one person. It can be as small as a group of two or three, or as large as an entire nation of millions of people.

A Mastermind that Affects Everyone

There are masterminds that currently interact with your dimension which affect each of you individually. Whether or not you realize it, you are immersed in masterminds every moment of your life.

Let us begin by exposing one of the strongest masterminds in existence. Many of you have been there—your casinos! If you have ever been to a gambling casino, you have not only participated in but helped strengthen one of the most powerful thought forms in the world. This is not something to be ashamed of, but rather it is an opportunity to understand and take advantage of it.

Let me share with you how the mastermind works. Talk to people headed for one of these great places of excitement and ask them how they feel about the journey. If you don't get at least one of the next few responses, then you may have encountered an exceptional individual who has somehow overcome the low vibration of this type of mastermind:

- Yeah, I'm going there to "donate" my paycheck!

- I'm only taking X amount of dollars with me, and when that's gone I'm quitting.

- I only allow myself to lose X amount of money per day, and then I return to my room.

- I don't know why I'm going. I never win.

- I know it sounds stupid, but even when I'm losing, I still have a great time.

I could go on, yet I believe the point is sufficiently made. Most people who enter gambling casinos are, for the most part, convinced that winning any real money is for the little old lady from Nowhere, USA, and not them.

How do you suppose such a mastermind got started, and how does it continue to dominate the reality of most who choose to experience casinos? It is a mastermind catapulted by the mass consciousness, convinced by the collective thinking that the average person will lose more times than not.

Although it does make for a good example, gambling houses are not the only places this belief system exists. The main reason I bring this up is that a very dangerous mastermind is forming at an alarming rate—that the world is coming to an end or that some devastating, cataclysmic event is about to take place. The only way to break such a mastermind is through a series of understandings:

1. Most activities on the planet are based on a mastermind.

2. Each thought pattern in the mastermind must be identified as a single aspect of the entire mastermind. Collectively, they are almost impossible to detect since they are deeply woven into your ideas and belief structures.

3. It is much easier and seemingly safer to be a part of, as opposed to being against, a mastermind.

4. Breaking a mastermind does not take a majority of the participants.

Most would agree that under current circumstances the people are not in control of their lives in politics. The same applies to the medical world, where you are "an illness waiting to happen," and treatment generally consists of damage control as opposed to preventive measures. Then there is the one that affects the masses called "poverty," which is a simple mastermind of lack. The list goes on.

Clearly, masterminds exist, and in some manner or other, most people play within the rules set by them. Masterminds can be broken, but it takes a will and a learned passion to train yourself to see them, and then to actually make them work for you.

Masterminding on a Conscious Level

The first step in creating a mastermind is to arrive at the clarity of what it is you desire in your life. This may appear to be a simple task, but for some—often on the subconscious level, the lack of clarity in thought is a way to maintain a sense of safety. Frequently, the distance that is created between your desire and your fulfillment is your fear of change. Therefore, it is equally important to recognize the reasons why you have not been able to fulfill these desires so that you may initiate changes to support your mastermind.

Once you have achieved the clarity of thought, you need to formulate it into a statement and express it in the now. This is important to remember, because in the past, you may have made a wish and continually repeated the desire in such a way to have it become a reality in your future. You will find that the subconscious mind works in mysterious ways, for if it thinks you are happy wanting something, it will maintain your reality of keeping you in the state of wanting—and never receiving. In other words, your subconscious mind may automatically assume that the desire to keep abundance in the so-called "future" is exactly what you want.

The next step is masterminding with like-minded individuals who are willing to become passionately involved in holding your vision of clarity. By collectively focusing on the desired thought, it will manifest in the now as opposed to in the future.

In recognizing the value of creating a mastermind statement that actually suits your particular needs, you will no longer seek the comfort of the masses. This is the true beginning of your ability to control your destiny, and in that, your truth is enlightened.

How to Adjust Your Life through Masterminding

You enhance your ability to advance your conscious reality when you choose to surround yourself with other evolving entities and mastermind together. Using the Trinity of Truth, Trust and Passion, you will begin to align the patterns of your soul to those in your group. This alignment creates a focused pattern of energy known as "reality," whereby the thought resonation of manifestation is clearly directed to move concurrently. Through masterminding in a collective energy, your thought can manifest and become your reality by the clarity of your focus.

For a detailed discussion of Sleepstate Programming and Masterminding, please refer to *Kirael: The Ten Principles of Consciously Creating.*

Glossary

A

Agape—The absolute, unequivocal vibration of unconditional love beyond the concept of yin and yang. Agape is the essence of love in its purest form.

Akashic records—A vibration of recorded events that span all time and space. It is said that these archives hold the histories of Earth and all other evolutionary systems.

All That Is—See, "Creator."

Andromedan—A being from the star system Andromeda. By appointment of the Galactic Council, the Andromedan society currently serves as the security force for the Earth plane.

Angelic realm (angelic force, angelic reality)—The dimensional reality of the angels.

Archangels—A high plane of angels assigned to an evolving system such as Earth. Usually the highest form of angel that will intercede on behalf of human endeavors.

Aspect—An energy pattern of the essential self, or higher self, focused into a specific realm of consciousness in order to experience a life plan. Typically, an essential self will incarnate three aspects of itself on one or more planes of existence, such as the Earth plane, at any given time. Alternately, the essential light may have aspects of itself manifest in other dimensions and/or planetary systems.

Astral body—The energy of Self. The astral body has the ability to temporarily discard the third-dimensional vibration and embodiment to become the wholeness of the energy of Self. It can travel without the pull of the magnetic forces of the Earth plane.

Astral travel—The act of traveling etherically—in spirit only, without a physical body. Traveling as a spirit energy in the astral plane of consciousness.

Atlantis—An Earth continent and evolutionary realm once inhabited primarily by beings of galactic origin. The Atlantean period of Earth evolution followed Lemuria and preceded the Egyptian era.

B

Beauty, the—The name Master Guide Kirael affectionately uses to refer to the Honolulu Church of Light, claiming it has a life of its own.

C

Carbon-based body—A physical life form, such as human, whose organic nature is based on carbon compounds.

Cellular consciousness—The conscious awareness and memories that are held within the cells of the physical body.

Chakra—A cone-shaped energy center in a physical body. In a common view of the human body, each of the seven major chakras is associated with a nerve plexus and has a unique color association: root or base chakra —red; sacral chakra—orange; solar plexus chakra— yellow; heart chakra—green; throat chakra— blue; brow chakra— indigo; crown chakra— violet. Each major chakra projected from the front of the body has a corresponding chakra projection on the back. (For a discussion of the evolving chakra systems, see Chapter 7, *Guide to the Unseen Self.*)

Channel—A connection between a human reality and the unseen forces of light (e.g., guides and angels) that facilitates the exchange of information. Also, a person who acts as a conduit for energy or information.

Channeling—The act of allowing ideas and information to flow from non-physical, non-human sources into the realm of human conscious awareness. See also, "Medium."

Christ Consciousness (Christ Energy)—The thought of the Creator. At the time of his baptism, Master Jesus became fully infused with and awakened to the Christ Light.

Collective consciousness—The combined awareness of two or more beings. See, "Mass consciousness."

Consciousness—A defined state of awareness.

Creator (God Creator)—The omnipresence of all Light in Creation. The essence of Love. The All That Is.

D

Dimension—A level of existence or consciousness.

Download—A large amount of information passed as a single parcel between the higher self and the ego-veiled human self, a process which usually causes intermittent breaks in the everyday thought system.

E

Earth plane—A description of the multi-dimensional entirety of planet

Earth as a staging ground where evolutionary processes can unfold.

Ego—The self-woven veil of thought that symbolizes the belief that humans and other forms of evolutionary beings are separated from the Creator Source. This veil of separation gives rise to limited thoughts as well as fears.

Energy pattern—Any being of light existing in a coherent state. Also, thought energy.

ET—An extra-terrestrial being. A non-human energy indigenous to other planets or planetary systems.

Etheric (ethers, ethereal, etheric fabric)—A reference to the living spirit force that permeates and surrounds all energy patterns (beings). The etheric fabric is non-linear space that cannot be divided linearly. There is no time-space continuum in the etheric space.

Evolution—The never-ending process of Creation: creating, experiencing and expanding consciousness. The process of developing an ever-expanding awareness of the Creator's Love. For example, moving through our human experience of the Third Dimension into another dimension of awareness.

Extra-terrestrial—See, "ET."

F

Fear—A self-created belief in a limitation used to control the self in order to experience a lesson plan. See, "Ego."

Four-body system (four bodies) —The physical, emotional, mental and spiritual energy bodies that comprise a third-dimensional incarnation, such as a human being or the Earth Mother. The balanced integration (healing) of these bodies moves you to a higher plane of consciousness.

G

Galactic brotherhood—A term used to encompass any form of evolutionary life existing outside of the Earth star system.

Galactic councils—Forerunners of a federation of galactic beings, empowered to reduce friction among developing societies.

God Creator (God Light)—See, "Creator."

Great Shift in consciousness—The evolutionary shift in awareness of the Creator's Love on planet Earth and within her inhabitants, moving the Earth plane from the Third Dimension into a new dimension of conscious awareness.

Guide—An entity of light that assists other evolving entities, such as humans, to move through journeys and evolve into a higher awareness of the Creator's Love.

Guidance Realm—The dimensional reality of the Guides.

H

Heal—To make sound or whole; to restore to health.

Healing—The process of making oneself whole. The understanding of your Oneness with the Creator. Complete healing takes place in all four energetic bodies: physical, emotional, mental and spiritual. See, "Four-body system."

Healing journey—See, "Journey."

Heart—The core of the Creator's essence within the Self. The Truth of who you are.

Higher self—Your soul. The spirit part of you that is constantly aware of all realities while still maintaining a continuous connection with your physical incarnation. Also known as the "essential self" or "essential light." A higher self is an aspect of a soul family that is processing on different dimensions simultaneously. (For a detailed discussion of the higher self, see *Kirael Vol. II: The Genesis Matrix*.)

Home (going home)—A description of the process of human death. Many believe that in this process they are simply returning "home" to the Creator's Light.

I

I AM—A biblical reference to the Creator Source in identifying its energy. This self-identification is used by many spiritualists as a key to centering one's focus on the pure intent of Self.

Illusion (illusionary)—A so-called "reality" created through thought for the purpose of experiencing a particular process or journey. The Third Dimension, which is a creation of collective thought, is an illusion.

Inward Healing Center—The organizational precursor to the Honolulu Church of Light.

J

Journey—The experience of following a chosen path. A collection of experiences or lessons planned by the Self for the purpose of experiencing and evolving itself on behalf of the Creator. In human terms, a journey is the process and the experience of healing back into the Creator's Love.

K

Karma—A set of life issues and/or lessons that you weave into your life's blueprint before and during an incarnation. When you choose not to handle a repeating lesson plan, your higher self will often give you the opportunity to heal the issue by placing it in the path of your life's journey. According to Master Kirael, "Karma is your right to correct your abilities, to keep a life plan totally aware of the Christ God Light." (See Chapter 4, *Guide to the Unseen Self.*)

L

Lemuria— An Earth continent and evolutionary realm where the Creator originally focused enough energy to set in motion human evolution. Lemuria was a heart-based society, where fifth-dimensional love existed. The remnants of the Lemurian continent can be seen as the Hawaiian Islands and landmasses around the Pacific Rim. From its inception into the Earth plane, the waters surrounding Lemuria immediately started sinking. The Shift is going to push the islands up into the air and add land mass.

Lesson plan—A rudimentary projection of what an evolutionary being would like to attempt to experience while incarnate. This plan may not always unfold exactly as planned, yet it gives the embodied life form a direction.

Light (Creator's Light)—The source and substance of All That Is. The energy of the Creator. The essence of Love.

Light being—An evolutionary, non-physical being.

Light body—A description of the human incarnate experience post-Shift, wherein the human body will be physically less dense at a molecular level, or more "light-bodied."

Love—The essence of the Creator that permeates all life throughout the Cosmos. It is the one force, Kirael says, that has no opposite. Love simply is.

M

Magnetic grid—The lines of energy that traverse the Earth between its poles. Because the Earth was designed as a duality experience it needed to be anchored by opposing poles.

Mass consciousness—The combined awareness of all human beings on the Earth plane. See, "Collective consciousness."

Masterminding—The act of creating a collective consciousness focused on manifesting a particular experience or outcome. This collective conscious can be comprised of physical humans, human essential selves, angels, guides and other unseen forces of light.

Mastermind (statement)—A thought form or mental construct held by more than one person. A mastermind statement is a declaration of either a desire or a belief.

Mastermind (group)—A collection of two or more people who come together for the purpose of masterminding. Masterminds can involve a few people, a whole nation or the inhabitants of an entire planet.

Material plane—The Third Dimension, an example of a physical realm of experience. A dense form of evolutionary light that allows for five-sensory, human experiences. At this level human beings can evolve through a journey of experiences.

Meditation—The practice of quieting your mind such that you are able to receive information, wisdom and guidance consciously. In Kirael's words, "Prayer is the asking; meditation is the hearing" of the answers to your prayers.

Medium—A human being who moves his or her consciousness aside and allows a spirit being to use the physical body to communicate with the human world. For instance, Rev. Fred Sterling is the medium for Master Kirael.

Metaphysics—An area of philosophy concerned with the fundamental nature of reality, being and consciousness.

N

90 percent (brain, mind or awareness)—Kirael refers to the human mind (or brain) as a two-part system: the linear, seemingly limited, third-dimensional, waking consciousness (the 10 percent) and the greater, non-limited, non-linear awareness of the higher self (the 90 percent). The "veil" or ego separates these two segments. As you evolve spiritually—expanding your conscious awareness—you gain greater and clearer access to your so-called 90 percent mind. Opening to the 90 percent through prayer and meditation allows one to move through the self-imposed limitations of the ego/veil to consciously hear answers and to receive guidance. The 90 percent combined with the 10 percent is the totality of your potential awareness, or your essential light. See, "10 percent (brain, mind or awareness)."

O

Om—A mantra consisting of the sound \om\ used in meditation and healing.

Over-mastermind—The ego/veil of Mother Earth. The mass consciousness of all humanity, especially the totality of all limited and limiting thoughts (i.e., fears) of the Earth plane. The collective belief that individuals have little or no control of their journeys or outcomes. Sometimes referred to as the "secret government."

Oversoul—The first accumulation of formed energy as it responds to the Creator's need to be evolutionary. From this level soul families are formed.

P

Passion—The core energy by which you feel the presence of your own Creator light. Passion is the realization that you are a limitless being of light and is the force that allows your life journey to continually evolve.

Photon Belt—The outer edges of spiritual-enforced Light particles, known as photon energy, which are moving into the path of Earth's sun system. This belt is so dense with light particles it is believed that when the Earth finally enters the fullness of this space, a form of darkness will prevail on Earth. It is said this passing density will occur over three Earth days; hence, the so-called "three days of darkness."

Pleiadian—A being from the Pleiades star system. The Pleiadian Empire consists of seven planets within the star cluster known as the "Seven Sisters."

Portal—An energy gate that leads us from one dimension to another. As one goes through a portal, the physical body is cleansed, electrons and metabolism are adjusted, the heart is realigned, and brainpower expanded.

Prana—In Hindu and Chinese traditions, the "breath of life." When pictured by intent as golden particles of Creator Light, this energy can be used and directed in many ways, including the energetic healing of the physical body.

Prana breathing—In the mind's eye, the practice of drawing golden particles of Creator Light into the physical being, most often through the crown chakra and pineal gland.

Prayer—The communication between your human self and your higher self, the Creator, and other unseen forces of light. It is an opportunity for you to define the life journey that you truly desire. In Kirael's words, "Prayer is the asking; meditation is the hearing" of the answers to your prayers.

S

Sirian—A being from the star system Sirius.

Sixth sense—Intuition and "knowing." Engaging the 90 percent mind through prayer and meditation opens the awareness of the sixth sense and opens your communication with the unseen forces of light. Human beings are not limited to the five senses; all have access to the sixth sense.

Sleepstate Programming—The practice of enlisting your own higher self or essential light to contact and communicate with the higher self of another during the sleep state.

Soul—A pattern of particle light, emanating from the Creator Source, that is in the process of evolving.

Soul family—A grouping of souls with a similar destiny. These beings of light choose to share incarnations in multiple realms simultaneously, collecting data that enriches the evolution of the Creator Source.

T

Table tapping (table tipping-)—A method used for divination or channeling whereby participants place their hands around a small table (e.g., a card table) and allow spirit entities to move the table up and down in response to queries.

10 percent (brain, mind or awareness)—Kirael refers to the human mind (or brain) as a two-part system: the linear, limited, third-dimensional, waking consciousness (the 10 percent) and the greater, non-limited, non-linear awareness of the higher self (the 90 percent). The "veil" or ego separates these two segments. As you evolve spiritually—expanding your conscious awareness—you gain greater and clearer access to your so-called 90 percent mind. Opening to the 90 percent through prayer and meditation allows one to move through the self-imposed limitations of the ego to consciously hear answers and to receive guidance. The 90 percent combined with the 10 percent is the totality of your potential awareness, or your essential light. See, "90 percent."

Third Dimension—A physical, material dimension of reality, such as the Earth plane. This dimension is based upon a duality system of "yin and yang" in which everything appears to have an opposite.

Third eye—The so-called "psychic eye" located at the center of your forehead. The energy center known as the brow chakra.

Trinity—The combined forces of Truth, Trust and Passion. Within this trine the Love of the Creator is anchored within the Self.

Trust—An inner knowing that comes from the Truth that you are part of the Creator and connected to all levels of reality. The understanding that everything in your life unfolds in perfection.

Truth—The essence of Love from which all reality extends and the basis of your light on Earth. The integrity of thought, word and deed that creates the freedom to be who you truly are.

V

Vibration—The frequency or frequencies of oscillation of all sound and light. Everything in Creation is a vibrating pattern of energy. All matter, thoughts and emotions are energies vibrating at particular frequencies.

Veil(s)—See, "Ego."

Y

Yin and yang—In Chinese philosophy the concept of two opposing principles (duality) which are basic to everything in the third dimensional reality. Yin is the feminine power, characterized by darkness, passivity and cold. Yang is the masculine power, characterized by light, activity and heat. The understanding that everything in the third dimension has an opposite, e.g., man/woman, hot/cold, up/down, right/wrong, etc.

Notes

Notes